ELINOR WYLIE
The Portrait of an Unknown Lady

Southampton, England

ELINOR IN 1910

ELINOR WYLIE

The Portrait of an Unknown Lady

by

NANCY HOYT

Illustrated

THE BOBBS-MERRILL COMPANY
Publishers

INDIANAPOLIS   NEW YORK

To

ANNE MACMICHAEL HOYT

ILLUSTRATIONS

ELINOR WYLIE
The Portrait of an Unknown Lady

CHAPTER

◇ I ◇

In January, 1883, the young couple who left a very High Church—St. Mark's, Philadelphia—entrained for their honeymoon.

They had a vague idea of using their two weeks which were allowed them by the bank for which he worked in mildly exciting expeditions to New Haven, Connecticut, and Cambridge, Massachusetts. For they were both young enough to have many college friends still dreaming in the academic sanctuary of post-graduate courses. But it was a snowy night and Anne MacMichael and Henry Martyn Hoyt, being at last free from Yale ushers, Harvard admirers, yards of Brussels Point, child bridesmaids, and clouds of rice and heavy incense, felt adventurous.

Quite unexpectedly, they left the train on which they were bound for honeymoon visits to New England at Bound Brook, New Jersey, and took a dilapidated sleigh to an even more remote spot, where a particularly beloved country cousin lived in the old dwelling which had housed many generations of the family.

9

At about half-past seven at night, Harry, pink-cheeked and rather shy, and Nancy, dark, glowing and romantic, knocked on the door of their cousin So-and-So's house. A surprised little girl let them in. They took off their coats; Nancy shook the snow and confetti from her fur pelisse. The much-beloved country cousins had heard all about the great wedding, but certainly had hardly hoped to have the bride and groom in person come stamping in from the night to the very early American parlor.

Mamma and Papa arrived in Somerville, New Jersey, on their honeymoon in 1883, and two years later, in a funny little wooden cottage, Elinor Morton Hoyt (Elinor Wylie) was born there, on September seventh, just as the oaks and beeches of the countryside were turning the russet and gold of her incredible hair.

As a matter of fact, the bride and groom had not been quite so rural and idyllic as to make Somerville their home immediately. They had experienced a frivolous and even luxurious two years in an apartment at Fifth Avenue and Tenth Street, New York. But the market crashed almost as spectacularly as in '29 and '73, a baby was on the way and both of them had a taste for trying the rustic charms of a cottage for two.

Elinor was born under completely unmodern circumstances. Both young people, naturally used to luxury, were rather more amused than distressed by this dove-côte of a house, which had only an iron stove in the hall for heat, an iron stove which the young father had to stoke every morning. The cold was so intense the winter after the baby was born that they often had to break the ice in the pitchers on the wash-stands. Heaven knows why such an experience did not kill a carefully cherished and intelligent banker's daughter, but apparently both my mother and Elinor throve on the experience. My mother and father were completely happy in the Somerville cottage with the baby, who already showed signs of being a wonder-child. My mother wiled away the time, when Papa was at work, by putting up wild strawberries and raspberries and talking to the friendly country cousins. Sometimes they went visiting, although it was a little difficult to drag the baby, aged six weeks, to Bound Brook and thence to Philadelphia, at the demand of young and adoring grandparents.

Finances became a little easier around '87, and they were moved (protesting slightly at leaving this happy backwater) to a suburb of Philadelphia, where a new baby, and then again another new baby arrived. The newcomers were Henry and Constance. Elinor was called "Big Hitter" by her much loved brother. He followed around devotedly in her trail, trying to copy her always precise methods of playing or gardening, or just existing. She was, even at five, a very slim, tall, proud child, with thick, dark amber hair and a straight, unfrightened gaze. All three of them were dressed in little washable frocks, something like those in the *April Babies' Book of Tunes* (by Elizabeth and her German Garden), so that in photographs, instead of appearing in the murky plaids and strange buttoned serges of the period, they do indeed look like three angelic children.

Elinor became so used to listening to her mother and father

11

and grandfather read aloud that she did not learn to read herself until she was nearly seven years old. It was a family much given to reading aloud, a habit, thank goodness, which they continued through my own youth. The youngest of the three babies used to complain slightly against Butcher and Lang's *Odyssey,* saying "I don't like that there Godyssey," but the older two gulped it all in.

Elinor went to kindergarten, and the sentimental teacher called her the infant Keats because she said, very romantically, that her mother's eyes were "like clear brown lakes, fringed with rushes," a slightly astonishing remark at the age of six. In fact, she was a prodigy always. Not many years later she chose as a birthday present from her grandfather a copy of *Hamlet,* bound in vellum, and signed by the great Doctor Furness.

In summer the family went to Mount Desert—Bar Harbor to be exact. It was not yet a resort of the rich, but an enchanting northern New England island, which Elinor never stopped loving, which she thought of when she wrote her loveliest lyrics, and which remained a living memory to her always. Very many years later she returned to live on Mount Desert Island and to make us all homesick with her writing.

Three-quarters of the year were spent at Rosemont, Pennsylvania, just outside of Philadelphia, where the three children, in spite of the fact that their young parents were not rich, enjoyed a night nursery, a day nursery, parallel bars, and other aids to the development of the purely muscular. Here they found the first snowdrops, crocuses and daffodils

12

ELINOR AGED EIGHTEEN MONTHS, VERY SOLEMN UNDER HER BEST HAT

and ran across to get strawberries and violets from the market gardener's family, who lived across the road. I am not saying they were brought up in an atmosphere of snobbishness, when I mention these crocuses, strawberries and violets, but they were really important things in the lives of the parents and three babies. Indeed, they cared about the same things other people cared about in the 'nineties. The children were down at the railroad tracks to watch the Limited to Chicago go by to the Columbian World's Fair of 1893, and to wave to their parents on the observation platform. This was one of the rare holidays my mother *ever* took away from them.

Friends from Yale and Harvard dropped in at the Rosemont place in the evenings after the babies were put to bed, ate everything in the house, talked until two in the morning, and departed curiously refreshed—mutual friends, such as the son of Samuel Morse, a young Ripley, not yet a professor, and other people who liked doughnuts and milk, and good talk.

From up-State Pennsylvania, the in-laws, my father's parents, would descend for occasional visits. And they demanded return visits to Wilkesbarre. On one of these trips to visit the Hoyts my mother temporarily succumbed to a virulent attack of typhoid fever. Evidently she was a pivotal point of the family, for Elinor could remember well her young mother's illness and the even stranger sequel—a trip to Europe for Mamma and Papa. The three children were left at Rosemont, while they two scampered across most foreign

13

countries, including Switzerland, on their first foreign *Voyage de Noces.*

My mother's parents, who made yearly trips to Europe, bringing back those thrilling garments and toys which remain ever in the mind as evidences of some almost unheard of prodigality, had also been terrified by this typhoid and its resulting weakness. Her father wished in every way to help both of them in the natural difficulties of life on a small income with three young babies. And so, one Easter, just as he was leaving, he gave my mother and father several hundred dollars to squander. Then he departed for Europe.

"Let's show the children Washington!" said my mother to my father. She had been there as a very young girl, a flapper, and had liked the old city. They grabbed the money, the three children, and rushed off for a week in the national capital, fully expecting to return to Rosemont, and, probably, from there to graduate into Philadelphia, the Assemblies, and the normal life of a married couple in America's most conventional city.

But my father, who belonged to one of the senior societies at Yale, met the nicest of all "Keys" men on the street in Washington, a Mr. John Porter, best beloved of his ushers and friends; and John, reminding him of the days when he had been a comparatively raw farmer boy with a certain disarming shyness, said, "Harry, why don't you come on with me and meet Mr. McKinley?"

So, on a week's escapade, after showing the children the more memorable pieces of marble around Washington, my father found himself Assistant Attorney-General of the United States, at the age of thirty-six. My mother, faced with the choice of a proved and known reality in Philadelphia or a chance of success for my father in Washington, took the chance. In 1897 they settled in Washington on K Street with all three children, to the horror of Philadelphia, a city which regards other localities as being practically uncharted, on no known map, and perhaps tinctured with malaria, yellow fever and leprosy.

Elinor started in at a school which has since, through many different phases, become the standard day-school of the city, Holton Arms. (It was Mrs. Flint's then.) I like to see the photograph of her on the school mantelpiece, when by some odd circumstance I drop into these halls where I was once a dingy child, covered with streaks of ink.

Almost at once the three children found their way around the strange and beautiful city, and became a part of it. In one of her later poems Elinor manages to convey, as no one else ever has, the impression of heat in midsummer Washington. Visitors to the city may feel this withering blast, but only the person brought up there really knows it.

CHAPTER

❖ 2 ❖

At sixteen, seventeen and eighteen Elinor was a blue-stocking, a very pretty and a very hard-working blue-stocking. She was passionately interested in her school work; aided and abetted by one of the head mistresses, she forced herself to all-night sessions before examinations and studied interminably, not with any desire to go through college but apparently for love of study. About the time of her last year in school she took black coffee upstairs to the bedroom adjoining that of her younger and more frivolous sister Connie. Connie remembered how she worked through the night by the light of a gas mantle, taking an occasional sip of coffee and going back to her books.

In 1903, just before she left school, she went up to visit her adoring grandfather, who was also her godfather and her companion in the discovery and appreciation of books. He took her to all the theaters, to an art show and to meet various young cousins. She wrote us that, although "Dada" was giving her a marvelous time and there were several good Sargents in the Academy show, she was crazy to get home.

She asked after the welfare of "the babies." (For Elinor always loved my brother and me without wanting to tease us as the other two children did. We were the two youngest, the unexpected ones, Morton and I. I was seventeen years younger than Elinor.) She wailed for her books and her school report; she wrote a classic and charming picture of Philadelphia for my mother's delectation, sent her love to my father and begged to be allowed to come home from the parties and Philadelphia to the pre-graduation hard work of her school in Washington.

Even at that time she was writing excellent, and classic, poems—a thing she would never have divulged to her teachers. They are not merely amazing as "Juvenilia," but are very nearly up to her finer lyrics.

And she was then almost as gifted in drawing as in writing. Drawing was her extra-curricular study; she was attending a life class at the Corcoran Museum of Art. When her mother asked her if the model had any clothes on, she answered, "Oh yes, two blue side combs."

She was slim and tall and shy. I think it was in a way lucky that Elinor did not remain blue-stocking and go to Bryn Mawr, because in spite of her erudition she somehow seemed to belong to pretty dresses and silk stockings, which at that time were not exactly the college girl's delight as they are now.

After she left school she must always have been dressed in pale pink and mauve with ruffly hats and sweeping parasols because that is the way I first remember her. We shared a

17

passion for pretty frocks, a passion which she always encouraged in me, even when my infant indiscretion led me to in-
sist on a lace and tulle bonnet one early spring, which gave
me an intense earache. There were rosebuds on that tulle and
lace bonnet, and the family gave me a little vase with doves
on it to compensate for the earache. I am glad Elinor had
the equivalent of that tulle bonnet even if her heartaches
were immensely complicated by it.

During the school years she had two best friends, one
named Ellen, a perfect darling who remained her intimate
friend until the winter of Elinor's death, although neither of
them had an easy life, and the other one named Yvonne, who
was one of those best friends who are also rivals in scholastic
attainments and looks and spur one on to greater attainments. Before she came out Elinor had no beaux, but several
admirers. Among them were a red-haired witty boy slightly
in disgrace with his own family, and a lame, intellectual
youth who went to church every Sunday in order to come
home with Elinor afterward and talk about books. The
lame boy's loyalty survived the alarms and excursions of her
future life. At eighteen she was slightly austere, although not
entirely free of flapper tendencies, because she did once go
to a fortune-teller to find out the future, and burst out laughing at the hair-raising events which he foretold to her un-
believing ears. But the fortune-teller was right—Elinor's
future was astonishing.

Mr. Shelley was already the "Subtle Spirit" that aroused
her greatest enthusiasm. There was never a longer and more

happy hero-worship than Elinor's worship for Shelley. Twenty years later, he seemed still to her to be her greatest friend. Twenty years later, in *Mr. Hodge and Mr. Hazard,* she may seem to use Shelley as a model for Mr. Hazard, but it was really herself. She did not mind having the influenza in London, but she could not have stood it for Shelley.

The graduation photograph looking so aloof has somehow, for all its youthfulness, an impression of dignity and maturity. Her mind was well-developed and adult at eighteen even if some of her reactions were still adolescent.

In summer the family usually occupied a number of rooms in a very simple wooden hotel at the end of North-East Harbor on that isle of the Hesperides, Mount Desert. The laundry bills of that era must have been terrific, for Elinor and her sister Connie and her girl friends wore long white linen sport skirts which swept the grassy paths and mud trails and were considered quite short because they were cut a half-inch off the ground. A fresh one was required every morning since the grass stains and the marks of lichen and moss had made the skirt of the day before impossible for any young lady to wear. Till she was seventeen she wore a flat black ribbon on her chestnut hair and usually she carried a book or painting things and sought out her favorite trails and mountain tops. It was a comparatively idyllic girlhood.

In the spring of 1903 both my sisters went with their grandfather on their first trip to Europe. He wanted to give them a good time, not instructive or educational but purely frivolous enjoyment. The girls, three and a half years apart,

19

which at seventeen and fourteen is a wider space than ever before or later, were happy together though they were very different in temperament. Connie, the younger one, was very neat and tidy and clear-headed; her top bureau drawers at home were smooth mosaics of little cardboard boxes with everything in place; Elinor's were wild collections of tumbled stockings, handkerchiefs and gloves. She was excitable and impulsive and would grab something she wanted, leaving everything else in a turmoil. Twenty years later she had become almost fanatically neat and spotless and finicking.

On the eve of sailing she lost all her keys and all her money, but as Constance had duplicate keys and Elinor was her grandfather's pet it did not much matter.

They had a lovely time in Paris, with lots of shopping for new clothes, presents for the family at home, theaters and wild little parties and drives in the Bois. Their portrait in pastel was done and sent home to Washington, where it still exists. It has a sort of history. It was done by a well-known and fashionable painter, but it is so ridiculously bad and was so unlike either of them that my brother Morton and I were bribed and carefully trained in later years to repudiate knowing who the two young ladies portrayed could possibly be. This, as the picture did not resemble them in the slightest, was easy. Even when they were there, in the room with the portrait, we could usually persuade inquiring visitors that none of us had the slightest idea of the identity of either pictured female. The artist had made Elinor quite stiff and stern and pink-nosed, and Constance had been drawn as a supine and slightly melancholy flapper with immense dark eyes. Elinor and I used to call it "Apoplexy and Anaemia." We became almost fond of it, the way one does of a lamp or a vase if it stays around for years and becomes a familiar object that is always good for a joke.

After Paris they went to London, and my grandfather took a suite on the Park side of the Hyde Park Hotel, which, in the early summer of 1903, must have been like a grand-stand seat, with all the ruffly and beparasoled ladies driving by in their carriages.

He took them to the Lyceum to see Sir Henry Irving and Miss Terry. They had often seen them in America—for Sir Henry was one of my grandfather's great friends—but this visit was more exciting. The glamorous host and his enchanting co-star returned the hospitality of Philadelphia with a delightful supper party after the play on the stage of the great theater. Bram Stoker, Irving's popular Irish personal manager and secretary, took a liking to Elinor and Constance. When he wrote *The Jewel of Seven Stars*, a thriller which came after *Dracula,* he dedicated it to both girls. They were of course delighted.

In late summer they came back to Mount Desert, where my mother had stayed with the baby (myself), happy with memories of a wonderful trip, but also happy to get home again to the family.

21

CHAPTER

❧ 3 ❧

THE OLDEST of a family, should she be a girl, has always
a little trouble in finding enough people for the first dinner
party before the debutante dance, which will end the sus-
pense as to whether she is going to be a success. Constance
had beaux from the age of twelve, devoted, loyal, admiring
beaux. Elinor had been lost with Shelley and Shakespeare for
so many years, that when, at the age of eighteen, she started
to come out (to the fury of her teachers, who wished her to
become a college graduate, or even a lady professor) the parents had the usual difficulty in scraping up enough young men.
Naturally, after that first dinner there was no trouble. Elinor
was completely lovely, but between the ages of fifteen and
seventeen she had perhaps preferred to encourage contem-
poraneous high-brows, rather than start in to work up a collection of partners for cotillions.

Perhaps she knew the cotillion partners would not be lacking. Certainly she never worried about elderly gentlemen between twenty-four and thirty-five, who gaped at her in the

22

street! Perhaps she went so far as to notice that some one of them looked like an interesting old person of, say, twenty-nine, but more than that she did not notice, as she was usually laden down with reference books (until she finished school) and the mental arithmetic that always goes on in the head of a prospective debutante.

All I remember of her coming-out party is a square of sticky green peppermint, a sort of Turkish paste, which was the specialty of Demonet's, and some things made of pastry, called "doormats," which were strictly not permitted in our diets. But I think I can remember Elinor, pink and white as a sea-shell, in coral tulle. If Mrs. Longworth really said that Elinor was "luminous and radiant" as a debutante, it must have been a wonderful description. (I saw the statement in the *Herald Tribune* this winter and cannot resist quoting it.)

Elinor was not languid or passive or frightened like that lovely creature, Jennifer Lorn, but she *had* been brought up "to wear frocks of fine Irish muslin, to tie blue ribbons about her waist, to go to church and sing hymns out of a velvet hymnal with a gold cross on it, to sit on a chair while her maid brushed her curls to splendour, to wonder drowsily why she loved cream-coloured roses better than yellow ones, and why she had ever been born."

About this time there occurred an interlude in a conservatory, almost as idyllic as the one in *Jennifer.* The tall, fair young man was just as much a person of race as many of Elinor's future sub-heroes, who are always subordinate to either Shelley or Lucifer. He was just such a person as one

23

would have expected her to marry. This fragile romance was conducted on technically classic lines from the rowboat above the cold emerald eel-grass of North-East Harbor, to the actual conservatory with pink and white striped curtains in Washington, D. C. Something happened; mildly embittered because this so suitable union did not occur immediately, Elinor rushed off and, without the knowledge of my parents, became engaged to a nice-looking and well-born young suitor with a bad temper, who had been courting her unsuccessfully for a year or more. The young man was perhaps twenty-five. His name was Philip Hichborn, and his father was an admiral.

I remember very little about their early marriage, except that he would keep her out all day in a very small and smelly motor launch, week in and week out, and she did her very best to like these outdoor amusements, though the broiling sun sent intense waves of pain through her head and burned her pale and rosy skin abominably.

In the next few years all that I can remember of the *ménage* (except that I was intensely jealous of their baby who was two years old when I was seven) was that they gave dinner parties almost every night, that the baby annoyed me, and that they had delicious sausages and griddle cakes on Sundays. Even after Elinor was a brilliant and lovely young married woman with a baby and a temperamental husband and a house most beautifully run, she did not seem to grow up. She still depended to an enormous extent upon her own family. It must have been hard for her to wear the

24

stiffly starched collars and the strangely cut garments which her husband's slightly crude taste dictated to her. . . . Philip died a few years later. I really remember him only as a very handsome boy, rather bad-tempered.

* * * * *

Halley's comet, arriving once every eighty years, could not have aroused more dumfounded amazement and utterly shocked horror, particularly among the worldly and gently immoral, than Elinor's elopement with Horace Wylie when she was twenty-four.

In the four years since she had come out most of the local society had been annoyed with her for her air of persistent virginity, her lack of vulgarity, her inability to join in the abuse of an absent person. She was as crisp and fresh as a crocus; her hair was spring-like and hyacinthine. Her complexion was apple-blossom, and her nature so annoyingly aloof as to make her practically useless as one of a foursome at bridge or a member of a local *cabale* engaged in destroying others' reputations. She seemed almost *too* virtuous.

The elopement crashed the mirror, not only of her own existence, but also that of at least eight or ten other people. To me, it seems more and more understandable; I feel she was a winged arrow, bound to be released at some sudden impulse from the bow of this world. It is difficult, in 1935, to understand how tremendously such an action disturbed three or four families and, temporarily, several cities. But in

25

1910, the little world in which we lived was shaken and frightened by the courage and decision of such clear-cut defiance. Only my mother, young but broken in health by my father's death, retained any sense of proportion about the whole affair. Other people, even Elinor's most intimate friends, if one can be said to have intimate friends at the age of twenty-four, babbled excitedly, and hid away in corners, terrified by the resonance of her early *finale*. For they thought it a *finale,* these friends. They were sure that Elinor was done for, socially, and they felt she had not the courage to form herself into a writer or painter. And so these rabbits (all neatly numbered in my memory) consigned her to oblivion.

Mr. Wylie was a great deal older than Elinor. Almost everyone felt sorry for Phil Hichborn, but at that time no one ever dreamed of being friends with both sides as people would now that frequent divorces have inured them to such situations. Mrs. Wylie would not grant Horace a divorce for many years. This made existence practically impossible in America for Elinor and Horace.

My mother's courage never faltered, although she was begged to give up speaking to Elinor or visiting her in Europe. It is Elinor who endures through her work and our memories of her. Even those who find this endurance irritating have contributed to it.

For ten years Horace and Elinor lived a life as inviolate as if it had been inside a crystal ball, completely absorbed in each other, profoundly uninterested in the rest of the world including even such friendly relations as my brother and my-

26

self. Theirs was a life so independent of people that their only needs were quantities of new and old books and a pretty cottage in any one of the southern Home Counties of England. They acted as if they had eloped to another planet. They openly held hands and mocked their former world. They were allies against everyone, and no other human was permitted inside their lines of defence. They were steadily and intensely happy.

Her little boy of two, who (after my father's death) had been left in the nursery with my brother Morton, then ten, and myself, then seven, seemed to her still there, being brought up as a younger brother with the happy companionship of two other children. As a matter of fact, due to the great changes wrought by my father's death and her elopement, the little boy was soon spending most of the time with his father's mother, and only part of his days with us.

Elinor was always reticent about the things she cared for most. She sent him children's books from England, through my mother, without putting inscriptions in them; but we knew they were meant for him and meant to be read aloud to him. . . . He was eleven years old when she saw him again. Anyone would hesitate to say how much they must have missed each other; their immediate mutual affection years later was a sign they had each felt a lack and an emptiness in an integral relationship.

CHAPTER

◦ 4 ◦

IN 1911 there must have been many unspoiled villages in the southern Home Counties of England. By some miraculous stroke of luck, Horace and Elinor chose Burley, not more than two hours from London by car, or fifty minutes by plane, but so remote from the point of view of casual travelers, that one had to take a train to Brockenhurst, change there and take another smaller train, then get out and be met by a car, if finances permitted, or by one of those traveler's carts described by Thomas Hardy. Burley will always to me be the heart of Wessex; the only local and yokel humor that I can bear is that of *A Few Crusted Characters*. But Burley meant something more than this to Elinor. It was a haven of refuge which would still be open to her today, as a famous and recognized poet, just as it was open to her in 1911.

No description of mine could explain Burley as well as Elinor's own. In a sketch called "Shelley's Grandson and Some Others," which came out in *The Bookman*, she spoke of it as "our fairy village, where nightingales sang in the

trees and the larks went up from the gorse in the common."
She was used to taking Shelley around the world and putting
him anywhere the fancy urged her, as if he were an around-
the-world aviator. She sends him through frontiers of early
nineteenth-century America, and again, when it amuses her,
she gives him a birthday party at Somesville, on Somes
Sound, attended by suitably exquisite young females. But
when she wished to write facts, even those facts had a glow
to them. Burley, she writes, was

"the most fairy-book place in the world, and I hardly dare
go back to England for fear it has changed! Of course, it had
Yew cottages and Rose cottages and, of course, those cottages, unlike suburban retreats, with similar pretty names,
actually had roses and yew trees growing in their gardens.
What is more, if they hadn't it was because the roses and yew
trees had died of old age, and had pansies planted on their
graves, not because the owners of the gardens preferred a
monkey puzzle and a magenta geranium starfish. The cottages had walls of cob and roofs of thatch, and there was a
grey church and a green churchyard, and a red and white inn
called 'The Queen's Head.' There were sherry glass elms
with rooks in them, and a beechwood that was pink and pur-
ple in April, and bright holly bushes which were covered
with scarlet berries in November. Unfortunately, by Christmas, the robins had eaten all the berries, but the robins
themselves, hopping about in the snow, did nearly as well.
They were small and plump and their breasts, instead of be-

29

ing the color of the mandarin oranges that you find in the
toe of your Christmas stocking, were the color of the very
reddest lady apples.

"In that village I ate clotted cream, and smelled wallflowers, and drank mead, all for the first time, and the cream
and the wallflowers were heavenly, but I am sorry to say the
mead was horrible.

"In this village there lived a lovely lady who was Andrew
Lang's first cousin, a gentleman who was A. H. Clough's son,
and a large, middle-aged gentleman who was Shelley's grandson. Of course he looked more like Shelley's grandfather.
The first two relationships interested me; the third shook
the aerial heavens of my mind. Think of it—Shelley's grandson, and I have had tea with him frequently! He was an
authentic eagle's feather; a somewhat small and whitish
feather, but still Shelley's grandson. He was also Harriet's
grandson, and I remember him looking impish and saying
gravely, 'You know, in this family we don't think much of
Mary.' I never dared ask him just how much he thought of
Shelley, nor admit the extent of my own worship, for as a
grandfather dear Shelley never had much chance."

That shows a little bit Elinor's fondness for Burley.

They lived in "Durmast," a thick white plaster cottage of
ridiculous antiquity, roofed in mossy tiles and thatch, surrounded by an acre of garden and two miles of heather on a
wild common, and infested by rats, which did not seem to
worry Elinor the least. In 1911, Burley (and please do not

confuse it with Beaulieu) was the heart of the New Forest, untouched by motorbuses and trippers.

A doctor and his wife, the rector of the church, a retired admiral, an intimate woman friend, and the Old Ladies were the calling list that any permanent inhabitant acquired. With this calling list and the fact of being a permanent inhabitant, went responsibility. Visiting the sick, distributing port and flannel petticoats and teaching Sunday School were part of these duties. Elinor was responsible, each autumn when the heather turned rusty, for the decorations of the tiny church's Harvest Home festival. Her hands painstakingly built the wreaths and long garlands which covered the chancel, while Horace was engrossed in loving Elinor, reading aloud to her, playing golf, bridge and chess, and finding out even more than he knew already about Napoleon.

The incredibly happy couple were known as Mr. and Mrs. Waring. The name grew out of a casual suggestion of my older brother's when, in hard pursuit of the eloping pair, he found them so happy that nothing more than a shrug and a little comprehension could handle the situation. Since he was so out of date in 1911 as to care for Robert Browning and quote him constantly, he said, "You have got to keep your own initials, and you assure me that you must change your name. Well, try Waring! I got the idea from, 'What's become of Waring, since he gave us all the slip?' Besides that there is the fact that you people wear your hearts on your sleeves, and something about the wearing of the green. Make it Waring!" And so they did for eight long years; in banks and golf clubs and on the lists of charities and when signing leases they were Mr. and Mrs. Waring.

I have often wondered why Elinor never wrote under the name of Waring, because as Mr. and Mrs. Waring such happiness as was theirs is seldom seen. With a shrewd and embittered eye, from the age of eight, I watched those two people and never for one moment did I see so much as a squabble. She is famous as Elinor Wylie, but do not forget that she was so happy as Elinor Waring that for six or seven years she ceased to write, except in her head, that instrument of precision which was as fine as any Swiss watch. Having thrown her bonnet over the windmill (and quite a windmill it was, in 1910) she let her heart guide her. And so, twelve years later, she would be writing in her prose work of the May (hawthorn) and the English countryside, not because she did not admire and love the American back-drop even more, but because the happiest years of one's life have a way of intruding themselves on later work.

Elinor was too happy to work. She taught instead, sang in the bathtub, composed poems on the way to church and could scarcely believe that in this sorry sphere such completion should be found.

When two people thumb their noses at the world, and leave a society as strictly arranged as a Buckingham Palace Garden Party, or a made-to-order corset, they expect perhaps a year of self-sufficiency, and always their ingenuous hope is that no one will find them or break into their crystal sphere of independence. What I find so amazing in Burley is that

when the inevitable wanderer who had once been an acquaintance in Washington turned up after two years, she made no
impression even when she spilled the beans and added insults
drawn from the inflamed imagination of dull people, who
thought to find a Lilith where there was only a still chilly
Botticelli Venus. These inevitable trouble-makers are never
lacking and must make life very difficult.

The rector, the doctor, their wives, and the Old Ladies
simply refused to listen to the malignant whispers, however
these whispers might upset Horace and Elinor. They decided
to move on, since their life was not dependent on the charm
and beauty of their surroundings, or the agreeableness of
their neighbors, but on each other. One could never tell if
they cared for you or not, because they seemed so independent
of all other human ties.

Long before this flitting was forced on them, my mother
and I arrived in October, 1912, and Elinor had ridiculously
lovely birthday presents for me. Her generosity was always
unbelievable, of mind and heart and hand. I was a shy and
precocious child, supposedly the only comedian in the family.
How the tangles and irritations of my life—considerably
complicated by the fact that Elinor had eloped and that my
mother was a young widow—how these irritations were
ironed out by the charming riches of the New Forest, which is
the oldest forest in the world, by the honey from Fortnum
and Mason's, by the sleepy village and its villagers, by the
rosy-cheeked happiness of Elinor, who insisted on dragging
me to Sunday School, only the New Forest could tell, and its

four-hundred-year beeches and elms tell nothing. I fell in love with the ponies, the wild ponies of the forest, which were only rounded up every two years. I was an abject slave of the Old Ladies and their Sealyhams, the first Sealyhams I ever saw. The Old Ladies, being Elinor's abject slaves, produced high teas suitable for a young lady of ten, and served them on their great dining-room table. There would be ginger snaps for Elinor, who liked those best of all, and toast for Horace, who was always slightly bothered by anything less than perfection, and the most exciting muffins and jam I have ever seen for me.

The air was cold, fresh and perfumed with the scent of the heather, frosty and rusting on the slopes of the common. Who cared about rats so long as there were ferrets to chase them and walls were three feet thick and four centuries old? There was a trivet stuck in the fireplace at tea-time, and the crumpets dripped butter. No telephone; scarcely any letters; I am not surprised that England often appears in Elinor's prose as an enchanted dream. Of course, she preferred America, its thorny charm, its incredible beauty; but she had to be grateful to England for the warm nest which was given her, when in flight against an entire civilization from a bad dream which might have brought madness to a mind less tempered, less cool, less sane than hers.

Always Elinor and Horace preserved a complete placidity, based partly on the love of the Burley inhabitants and their reciprocated love. It was for fear of injury to the tranced beauty of Burley, of tarnishing by even a touch the devotion

Philadelphia

AGED FIVE AND ONE-HALF. WITH THE ALPHABET AND A BUNCH OF THE
FIRST ARBUTUS

shown them by its people, that they left and went off to Hampshire. When they left, Elinor had become a firm friend of Shelley's grandson, and the lasting intimate of three or four people who lived there. Again and again they returned. The holly trees, the black thorn, the heather, and the inhabitants claimed them a thousand times. In retrospect, it seems a shocking waste that they should have been hounded out of their completely suitable cottage, which loved them with that half-psychic sense which an inanimate object can give to its owners.

Had it not been for this stupid acquaintance from the past in Washington, Elinor would have known only the New Forest, its strength and its beauty. Other stragglers from that past, particularly those who knew her before her elopement, did their level best to drive her from pillar to post. Moved on and hustled away by the stupidity of these malicious stray souls, buying a cottage here and a house there, she managed to cover a great deal of territory in the more beautiful of the English Home Counties.

But should anyone think that England was the only country to which her heart turned, I suggest that they read her poem, "As I Went Down by Havre de Grace." In it there is enough to make an American citizen of almost any alien who trembles lest he acquire a crude country without feeling or tradition. Her compliments and much of her love were for England; her instinctive feeling was for the United States. Later on, she felt she belonged to both.

CHAPTER

⋄ 5 ⋄

E LINOR, walking along the edge of the Burley common past the shy rabbits and the easily frightened furry ponies, was perhaps too happy to write a great deal of poetry. But she read it continually, thought about it always, and perhaps she was, in a way, living it.

About that time she found a small and very exquisite edition of Blake's *Songs of Innocence,* so beautifully bound and so perfectly printed that the little book, as well as its contents, gave her great pleasure. She presented this to her mother, who as usual was spending some weeks with her, and then they decided to gather together her own poems and have the same house print them in approximately the same format. In the last few years, from time to time, she had added a poem or lyric. The arrangement of the verse was her own. My mother paid the bill, which was small considering the beauty of the little book. I think originally sixty copies arrived at Burley from London. Some were given to English friends. Years later she let certain New York intimates

36

have a few copies, but it has never been on the market.

It is a small, square book with stiff cardboard covers, lovely paper and perfect type. The title is *Incidental Numbers*. (I could not understand that name at the tender age of nine.) It is unsigned, but beneath each poem the date when it was written is printed. It was made in London in 1912 and, although privately printed, must stand as her first book because of the high quality of the work in it. Between those grey-blue covers a reader finds a great deal of her youthful heart and early years. Elinor liked the feeling and the look of the little book. I think she was slightly thrilled by its small perfection, just as later the first edition of *Nets to Catch the Wind* gave us all that same sense of pride and astonishment that a very new baby gives to its parents.

And all the time she was reading everything new and a great deal that was old. A box of books came down weekly from the lending library.

Horace and Elinor traveled a lot in France in the time before the war, because neither could stand uninterrupted years of England, roast lamb and the illustrated weekly magazines. They loved England, but they were slightly touchy Americans in voluntary exile, so that if their national feelings were irritated, they went motoring to Pau, or dined in unexploited French restaurants, or Elinor would refresh her spirits with several new Paris dresses, which were quite unsuitable to quiet evenings in the English countryside. In Burley, a few tweeds and Liberty tea gowns were the correct equipment for many years of wear.

Had she not been so cool and pink and happy, and Horace apparently contented with a country life of golf, bridge and occasional motor drives, I would say that she must have seemed an exotic flower to the people around her. But she did not. I fancy both of them were lonely for America, but before war time it was an easily assuaged loneliness. It is only after war breaks out that one finds any other country intolerable.

One of our classic amusements was "Writing to the Stores," a pastime which must still hold good today because Miss Delafield's Provincial Lady does it so frequently. Interminable correspondence arose, and I much approved of this way of conducting all shopping because the samples and scraps of flowered silks and lawns were my perquisites for small dolls' dresses. Kewpies were just beginning, and the samples were quite large enough to make them elegant creations. People who dropped in at tea-time might find Elinor dressed as a sort of Alice-in-Wonderland in one of my frocks and looking about eleven years old, while I would be in her most elaborate brocades and as much made-up as one palish-pink lipstick and a piece of charcoal would allow. Sometimes we paid return visits to country houses, for which we cared less because I was sent to visit puppies and kittens in the stables and Elinor was obliged to be very grown up in the drawing-room and discuss the new Rector or the lateness of Holland tulips with our hostess.

Life had not altered in 1912 from John Leech's England. People made the most awful howls about putting stamps in their housemaid's Insurance Books and everyone joined in cursing out that dangerous new fellow, Lloyd George. A parlormaid cost one hundred and thirty dollars a year or a little more if she were "tall, slim, Church of England, able to valet gentlemen and good at knife-cleaning." If she were a nice girl, her employers gave her a dress at Christmas; if their enthusiasm was not aroused, she received an umbrella. (One wonders why she did not learn knife-throwing instead of knife-cleaning!) Naturally, munitions and munition wages were to change all that.

Elinor was accustomed to reading the best books, wearing the nicest tea gowns, and living the most quiet of quiet lives. After Burley, we moved to Thruxton, to a thick plaster house with a thatched roof and one of the most amazing gardens I have ever seen—a garden heavy with the scent of flowers from spring to late fall, a garden blue and gold with forget-me-nots, massed thickly like enamel around a bed of sweet elyssium.

The wild woods of Thruxton were thickly sown with blue-bells, hyacinths, daffodils and crocuses. In the village street, an automobile created more excitement than the airplanes from Farnham winging overhead. Here at least was a stopping place between Burley and the house which she had almost literally to defend for the next four years. There were bees sticky with honey at Thruxton, almost too much asparagus for any one family to eat. Yet above the tranquillity of the village loomed the shadow of war. In the weekly book box from the Lending Library a volume arrived,

39

succinctly titled *The Next War,* by Bernhardi, and since our sister Constance (Baroness Stumm) was married to a German, and all the rest of us were openly against any form of combat, we shook in our boots. As a temporary measure, since Connie was to be in the German Embassy in Brussels, it was decided that I should enter a convent school there and learn French. The thought of a Belgian convent was terrifying to me—as perhaps to any eleven-year-old child. Elinor, always the ally of the childish mind and of those who are frightened, promised me that I would not have to go to this convent school. My courageous mother disbelieved in the ridiculous rumors of war. There would be no war; it was simply out of the question! We would be quite happy in Brussels near Constance.

Elinor and Horace, wanting more room, moved the next spring to "Lascombe," Puttenham, Guildford, Surrey—such a very long address that I made up a song about it.

Elinor and I walked a lot around Lascombe in a small radius, as far as her vitality, for she was not very strong that summer, would allow her to go. One of our favorite ways was across two fields and down a steep pasture to some great trees, under which sat one of our very best friends. He was an old shepherd, with a grey beard, and the ingenuous eyes of kind maturity, which still held a certain childishness. His patience was inexhaustible, and his capacity for enjoyment was illimitable, although his life was channeled in the narrow path between the farm buildings and the pasture. He had an assistant whom he regarded as a raw, though willing, boy of about twenty-five, and those two shepherds had their counterparts in the two sheep dogs, huge, woolly grey things, called English shepherds, over here, who helped them attend to a very large flock. There was an incredibly kind and astute dog named Bob, of perhaps eight years, and, in training, a more excitable bundle of grey worsted, nearly three years old, called Jim.

Elinor and I, in big straw hats from Liberty, bound in flowered muslin, and adorned with long velvet streamers, would start out for a few minutes' ramble, and we would end up sitting for hours, spell-bound, next to the old shepherd. He and the elder dog were amenable to the charms of milk chocolate and slightly jealous of any chocolate which went to the younger shepherd or the younger dog. His stories, told with an indescribable charm, were somehow never boring. Half a mile away on a hillside we could hear the click of horns and skulls, as two rams contended over some unusually charming ewe. The shepherd would nod at the older dog, and in a moment Bob, a huge animated mass of grey worsted, would go bounding up to police the refractory parties, and stop the row. It was a marvel to see these dogs round up the sheep, hundreds of them, and take them home at night through the narrow way of hedged lane, back to the byre.

One day in July, our darling old shepherd showed intense excitement. He was unable to talk of anything except a military tattoo at Farnham, which was to take place next week, and which his employer was going to help him attend.

41

Although Elinor and I were interested in hearing about it, we could hardly understand why he was so excited.

"Tha knows, ladies, as th'ull be my first day off in twenty-two years!"

"But what about Christmas?" said I, aged eleven, still counting that the greatest of all treats. "What about Sundays? Don't you ever get off?"

"The sheep be needing me just as much Christmas and Sundays as any other day, missy. But the master thought as how Bob and Jeff," he indicated the young shepherd, "could manage just for the afternoon without me next week. So I be going to Farnham, and seeing all they soldiers and aireoplanes go flying overhead."

It really was his first holiday in twenty-two years, and he was infantile in his anticipation of joys to come.

Elinor and Horace had bought a house at Witley, Godalming, in June, 1914, and through July we would go over there from Lascombe. While I wandered through the raspberry canes, yellow raspberries which tasted of sun and sweetness, they would go up and direct the workmen, who were painting and plastering the inside of the rosy brick house, seventeenth century and terraced and somehow lovable, but in a great need of what were even then known as modern improvements. There was a sixteenth-century school-house, near by, used as the gardener's lodge. There were trees and a lovely garden in back. Below the terrace were the strawberry and raspberry beds and a few flowers. The whole thing was walled by the same rosy brick, and a little rivulet bounded it on one side.

Witley is a sort of adjunct to Godalming, which is in itself one of the scattered pearls around the annoyingly suburban-smart Guildford. Witley is a very small village indeed, and I strongly suspect Godalming of being Kipling's "The Village that Voted the Earth Was Flat." In that story, the locale and local police, the magistrates and the sleepy stupidity of the place are perfectly described. I do not *think* that that story is about Godalming; I am sure it is.

As this book is not supposed to be heroine-worship, I may say a funny thing about Elinor. Having borrowed money from my mother to buy the house at Witley, she started out with the best intentions; she meant to reserve the very finest bedroom with the nicest outlook for my mother, and the little one next to it for me and the nurse, who had once been her own maid. But as the workmen progressed, she somehow could not bear to part with the nicest rooms, which became in her mind's eye study, or boudoir, or workroom, and finally, I think, she assigned us two strange little cupboards over a staircase.

CHAPTER

⌗ 6 ⌗
―――

EUROPE was in its fine flower in July, 1914. There were
hobble skirts, dyed wigs, good manners and bad ethics. The
United States came into these things only as an observer.
We perhaps were more involved than other families, since
we had a sister married to a German. But such a nice German, such a quiet and intelligent German! He still is all of
that.

My brother Morton arrived—with the mumps—alone on a
huge ocean liner at Southampton in July, 1914. Four weeks
later he and I were lying out on the grass in one of the many
pastures around Lascombe listening to the English airplanes
buzzing overhead, while we made futile gestures at them to
descend and take us to the scenes of combat across the channel.

A moratorium had been declared on all money. We could
not hear from the sister who was married to a German diplomat, a diplomat obliged to do a lot of the dirty work connected with the German ultimatum to Belgium. We barely

44

knew how to get into communication with our own embassy. Elinor remained comparatively unruffled throughout these troubles.

I must say that Morton and I hoped our services would be needed at any moment on the Allied front, although we were singularly untrained young persons of fifteen and eleven. Our one idea was to get back to America, and try to keep it out of war or, if the worse came to the worse, to bring it in on the Allied side. Elinor's problem was more involved. She could not very well go back to the United States; she could not very well stay where she was and keep her family around. She could only try to keep a cool head and a warm heart.

Besides any mental tumults, Elinor had the constant irritation of a bad leg. We all thought of it as "Elinor's bad leg." A small wound, incurred accidentally, had refused to heal. Horace, always extravagant in his desire to take care of her, had consulted the greatest doctors in Europe to cure it. It would be impertinent for me to say that the long, hidden homesickness for the United States was one of the chief reasons why the wound did not heal, but when I remember the trained nurses, the doctors, the surgeons, the great men of Harley Street, the titled specialists, the imported physicians from the Continent who came and looked at that small mark on her slender shin, when I think of all these people and realize that two months of exposure to ordinary American sunshine cured the leg definitely and finally, I must say, even if I *am* considered impertinent, I feel that that wound was the wound of homesickness. Why else should an open

45

wound, incurable by every great doctor in Europe, be cured when, by the turns of politics, the war drove Elinor and Horace home? Seven or eight weeks of sunshine changed Elinor from an invalid, attended by two nurses and two doctors, to a beautiful and husky young woman.

How and why she arrived home, I am going to try to tell you, because it is really dependent upon those huge political movements which are called war. We were all of us living in a big house outside of Guildford when war broke out. There was my mother, Elinor, Horace, Morton and I, comparatively happy and harmonious, although Morton and I would have liked a little more excitement.

Those English novels which start with "It was a beautiful day in Surrey in July, 1914," remind me of the placid boredom of that month before chaos. Except for the amusement of playing with the live stock and the two cats, the pleasure of picking strawberries and mushrooms and counting the planes overhead, ours was an uneventful existence, relieved from complete tedium by ten bound volumes of *Punch,* and *The Encyclopædia Britannica.*

The war started off unexpectedly. To ordinary English people it was like a giant cracker set alight under their noses. Within two months a state of unparalleled hysteria prevailed on the continent, and England's old maids turned into vicious spinsters, relating stories about trains of Russians passing through country stations, the imminence of food shortage, the likelihood of all German atrocity tales, and other horrors.

My mother wanted to get home to America with the two

46

children, but the ships were being used for transport service. Money was difficult to obtain, and all the waiters suddenly became funny old men with dyed mustaches, as the young German waiters had rushed for their fatherland and the young Englishmen were joining Kitchener's first army.

Strangers were not wanted, but there seemed no place for us to go. Still, we tried to go. We chartered three taxis, and our hegira took us across three counties to hospitable Hampshire. There we found a little group of Americans, caught by the war, marooned in Bournemouth, a seaside resort, although many United States citizens would have gladly crossed steerage to get home.

About twenty of us stayed there. The children of the group, at least, vastly enjoyed the sunshine, the lovely weather, and the inner scene of danger and excitement. There was only the English Channel between us and the front—a convenient, if temperamental, bit of water. We could hear the guns on a clear day, or at least we thought we could. People did not insult us so much or feel quite so suspicious of Americans as they had in a tiny community, although my brother, who was tall and just fifteen, and a boy from Philadelphia, who was tall and fourteen, were each handed white feathers for being slackers.

It seems silly, these managed and arranged dislikes which grow up as side issues to senseless carnage. Elinor and Horace were so pro-Ally that I believe Morton and I became childishly annoyed by any dispatches at all. Of course, one read only what one was allowed to read in the daily papers. How-

47

ever, Bournemouth *did* take us away from the spinsters with stories about regiments of Russians and threw us with our compatriots. It was a little like being on a desert island, and at eleven, that is a satisfying existence.

Passports did not exist for Americans in western Europe in 1914. But somehow, my mother managed to get room for us on a boat bound for New York in October. The portholes were darkened, the ship sailed from Liverpool instead of Southampton, lights went out early, and many passengers went around with a life-preserver look to them, as if at any moment a submarine would scuttle us. So we went home and left Elinor, not because we wanted to, but because she preferred to stay in England until things cleared up (which would be a matter of months), until the war was over, and she could be legally married to Horace by the complicated laws which govern our lives in the states of the eastern seaboard.

They not only stayed on, but they bought and furnished a house, and Elinor did war work and knitting and outfitted bewildered and ungracious Belgian refugees. It does not sound like her novels, but Elinor, by the time she wrote those novels, had attained a satirical outlook on life. Sometimes I wish she had written just one book in those years when she was very young and impulsive. It might not be as finished as her later work, but it would not seem groping or unfinished. She never did. She could not write badly. And speaking of that modern novel which she never wrote, I am constrained by a regard for the truth to tell something about

Elinor which shows not only that she was a writer at twenty-six, but was also (for a writer) incredibly patient and of a forgiving nature, a characteristic which I, myself, cannot understand.

When she was twenty-five, she started a novel, which was to be anonymous. There was a most amazing opening chapter, in which a young girl and her best beloved on an elopement arrive in Paris. She was able to evoke Paris at night—the wet, black streets shining; the cab driver in his linoleum-covered hat, the glowing lights on the bridges, and the luxurious sanctuary of the hotel, all written from the point of view of a very young woman, unused to the foreign scene. The girl she was writing about was herself; she was recording her own early impressions. After the beginning in Paris, several more chapters were completed. Elinor wrote them in Burley, and because she must secretly have longed for a reader, and for critical comment, she posted them to Constance, who was at the time, 1914, everything that was most correct as the wife of the Second Secretary of the German Embassy in Rome. Constance read the first chapters, liked them very much, and lent them to another American girl, married to a foreigner. Several weeks later, when Elinor asked for the return of the manuscript, so that she might continue work on it, these young American ladies in Rome blandly stated that they had lost it. What this meant to Elinor at the time I can scarcely imagine. I should think she would have torn her pretty chestnut hair out by handfuls. It was her first real book. She had worked hard on it, and the only existent copy in her own handwriting had been lost somewhere in the complex shuffle which went on in Rome just prior to the World War. It was eight years before she started another novel, but I never heard her say anything disagreeable about the loss of that book.

Of course, she was always generous both in heart and in mind. I can remember arriving as a spoiled child of eleven in the summer of 1914, and telling Elinor in a most annoying way that my other rich and beautiful sister gave me nicer presents. Elinor, always childish, gave me one horrified look, ran into her bedroom, and returned with her skirt full of every toy and bauble she had accumulated in the previous few years. My conscience was so burdened by this atrocious baiting of Elinor that I persuaded her never to tell another soul about my ill-judged remark.

She was fond of cooking, and very good at making strange and wonderful concoctions in a chafing dish, which were an extremely welcome relief after weeks of mutton and cabbage. I do not know why she should have been unable to sew, and yet have been such a good cook. I have even seen her produce difficult little cakes, called "sand tarts," and as for more elaborate dishes, they were translated by her hands into poems in food! She never lost this ability to cook.

They were settled in the house at Witley by the winter of '14, and stayed there two years. Soon there was a camp of soldiers near by, and Elinor was doing war work for a beautiful lady in London, knitting scarves for somebody else, and serving on the board of war charities. War is a curious thing.

The first thing it stops is normal communication. Even when somebody has lived in a place for years, and is known by everyone, after war starts, trouble begins to brew for him. I have seen an American lady in America, excited by war fever, try to arrest her own second cousin as a German spy. So warped and tortured do people's ideas grow under this abnormal strain. Although happy and much liked by the community, Elinor and Horace began to be asked for passports and papers, and were looked on with slyly suspicious eyes by outsiders. By the late summer of '16, the situation became intolerable. They sold the beautiful house which they loved so much, and came back to the United States. We had expected the usual weekly letter from England; instead we heard by telegram that they had arrived in Boston.

Because Elinor cared for trees and sky and hated close confinement, they took an apartment on the Fenway, far from the center of things, but at least affording a park where she might walk.

She never looked prettier and she had begun again to write poetry. She would compose poems in a bathtub or in a museum, and they went straight from her head to the paper. Later on, she wrote novels this way, typing out scholarly and even stilted pages without the need of changing a word, amending, or using a reference book. Her long years of absorbing had made her a polished instrument for creating.

My mother immediately asked her up to Mount Desert Island, at the northern tip of Maine, and it was while she was staying at our cottage at Bar Harbor that she re-discov-

51

ered Somesville. Somesville is a sprinkling of Neo-Greek cottages, very Palladian, with a small classic church along a road which wanders beside the fjord-like Somes Sound. A band of settlers from Massachusetts, equipped with a Bible and a book of Greek architecture, had settled there more than a hundred years ago. The ridiculous, mature beauty of the spot, paralleled only by Como, Maggiore, Capri or Tahoe, with the purple-blue mountains rising straight out of the blue sea, has a classic precision. These little white cottages in Somesville have pediments and columns decidedly Greek in their design. This, added to the natural charms of white shingles and wine-glass elms, is somehow breath-taking in its simple beauty. Elinor rented a sea captain's cottage, which had reddish-brown inlays of mahogany paneled in the walls, made from wood the captain had brought back from the West Indies in his clipper ship.

Somesville had been one of Elinor's favorite resorts as a girl, when with her brothers and sisters and friends she had made excursions to the Somes House, one of those white wooden, ramshackle buildings which in northern New England pretend to be hotels. The Somes House was famous all over Mount Desert Island for its popovers and crab-apple jelly. At that time the popovers were brought out onto the porch and served in batches just fresh from the stove. The existent record for consuming them was made by a fat young friend, who managed to down sixteen of these airy objects. So now, years later, when Elinor fell in love with the sea captain's cottage, she did not feel strange, since it was only a few hundred feet away from the very float and path where she had come so many times, years earlier.

They did not have a great deal of money to spend, and so a little paint, some wallpaper and a great deal of taste went toward refurbishing the inside of the cottage. In the long butter-colored dining-room there was an enormous fireplace with a little oven at the side built into the bricks, the kind of oven one still sees in places like Mount Vernon. It was used as a repository for books, handkerchiefs or manuscript poems, because a more practical age had tacked on a small kitchen next door. There was a barn with lots of apple trees around it, and yards of sweet peas which never seemed to stop blooming.

When they were established in the sea captain's cottage, my little nephew, Philip, who was her only child, arrived to spend the summer with us. He was a gay and destructive little fellow of eleven, not unlike "Penrod." (Now, at twenty-six, very grown up and poised, he laughs over his exploits at eleven.) The first day he arrived in the Bar Harbor cottage he managed to break the player piano, stall the cheap little car we owned, and somehow dislocate the pump belonging to a spring in a Mount Desert forest. It was, however, a happy summer for him. He spent some time in Somesville with his mother, occasionally overnight or a week-end, when she satisfied some obscure need of his for hero-worship, as well as that ordinary affection which my brother and I—almost too familiar figures, both of us gawky adolescents—were unable to give to this youngest member of the family who has

53

always seemed more like a kid brother than like a nephew.

Elinor would wander along with one of her favorite books; she and Horace would picnic on some upland pasture overlooking the sea; and her long homesickness came to an end and a fruition, for she began again to write verse, this time those poems which we love so well. It would be a satisfaction to any discouraged writer—with a genuine gift—to realize that at first Elinor's finest poems were several times refused. There were two exceptions. Miss Harriet Monroe of *Poetry* in Chicago accepted four of them and put them aside for later publication; and *The Century Magazine,* at the time a fairly prosperous member of that self-consciously correct collection of magazines known as the "Quality Group," was interested at once. I think *The Century* was the first to publish two of her poems, and they paid on acceptance!

She was always without any form of physical fear, although her spirit winced at slights which she learned to know well. She did not mind motoring through the most intense thunder storms with lightning flashing from one mountain to the other like a scene on the stage. She suffered continually from intense headaches, but seldom complained.

Another thing besides the actual love of the place which endeared Mount Desert to Elinor was that two or three women friends, who, among many deserters, still continued to be loyal, unchanged and affectionate, lived there in summer. It must have seemed extraordinary to her to have two or three friends instead of dozens, but she was not unhappy. She was very fond of coming over for dinner to my mother's

54

house on the other side of the Island and we paid many return visits. This was during the summer when there were a number of visitors and temporary residents on the Island.

But when the winter comes to northern Maine it is a thing of strength and fury and power. The temperature stays well below zero, the roads are deep in hard snow, and sometimes even the salt water freezes over. All the summer butterflies disappear around September, and by late October winter is there. The Island must be incredibly beautiful under the mantle of snow. Elinor and Horace refused to leave it. Instead, they closed their cottage at Somesville and rented a warm little apartment over a grocery store in Bar Harbor. It was in those rooms that she wrote such lyrics as "Velvet Shoes," "Sea Lullaby," "Winter," and "Fire and Sleet and Candlelight."

They became a part of that tiny snow-bound community. Elinor's eyes were never strong and until that winter she had never seen a movie, but she went to the bi-weekly shows quite happily with the rest of the population. In January, Horace became worried over her health, and they left their igloo for the South.

They went to Augusta, Georgia, and took rooms in a boarding house where, under the beneficent southern sun, Elinor's vitality quickly returned. She made great friends with the children of the boarding-house owner. She acted in little plays with them, helped them with their lessons. In return they took a full sheet of what are colloquially called the funny papers or, to be more high-brow, the comic sheet,

55

choosing, I think, *Polly and Her Pals* and named one of them "Mr. Wylie, a man to be respected, a spouse." They then labeled Polly—the prettiest picture they could get of her— "Mrs. Wylie, beautiful girl, actress, mathematician, poetess." This was presented with much homage to Elinor. I think the whole thing annoyed Horace a little bit.

It was the era of knitting for oneself and for one's brothers who were going off to fight. Horace was too old to join and Elinor was about fed up with war after her experience in England. There seemed almost literally no place to go, and partly because Washington was far the most difficult job to tackle, they most perversely insisted on living there. They had now been married legally for about two years. The ceremony had taken place in Boston amid loud giggles from both of them, with no onlookers present. Before that Elinor had been a widow for some years. It was Horace's wife who had made the legal tie impossible for so long, a thing which was considered angelic in the early part of the twentieth century, and now might be recognized as spite-work. One must remember that Horace had had to resign from all his clubs in 1910, and Elinor had no friends left in Washington except us, the family, who I think were half nuisance and half companionship for her.

My mother found them a little house on Florida Avenue, and Elinor's same household gods were set up there. The eighteenth-century Sheffield mirror, with candlesticks and clusters of silver grapes, the fruit and flower still-life, the Wedgwood lamps, the blue velveteen sofa, the strictly Palladian simplicity of her eighteenth-century chairs and the hot sunlight pouring in the windows transformed the little triangular-shaped room into an attractive sanctuary.

Sinclair Lewis, a college friend of my older brother, and his wife had a tiny house in Washington that year, and in between his writing of *Main Street*, which was a new departure for him, he and Elinor would argue for hours about writing and laugh about the ridiculous stupidity of some people. "Red" Lewis had a great sense of humor, even a slightly savage one. He must have been one of Elinor's first contacts with literary people.

CHAPTER

◦ 7 ◦

Washington in war time and in the two years following was a strange bureaucratic city. I do not deny that new
persons prejudiced against it can with justice say that it is
always a strange bureaucratic city, but toward the end of
the war housing became difficult and harmless householders
found themselves billeted with war-workers who not only
had quite different habits from the house owners, but often
had new babies as well. However, Washington never loses
its outward aspect of beauty. Elinor had no extra rooms, and
I think she enjoyed walking around the town at a tremendous
pace, in a black one-piece frock, much shorter than she had
ever worn since her school-days, and helmeted like a female
Mercury in one of the first of the close-fitting hats which were
to be standard for the next ten years.

Finances were extremely difficult at the moment, for she
and her husband had borrowed just a little more than my
mother could afford to give them for the Witley house in
England and they had sold that house in war years at what

58

is known as a knock-down price in order to get back to the United States. This left them with small capital, and that melted pretty quickly. Elinor lived simply, surrounded by pretty things, and wrote poetry furiously with practically no hope of any financial gain. As for Horace, he managed to find a job in the Interstate Commerce Commission in the one city where all signs and portents seemed to be against him. He had literally no pull, no helping hand, no advisers. But in a competitive examination this man, almost fifty years old, used to an open-air life and the study of chess and Napoleon, managed to pass the rather stringent requirements very well and was rewarded by a position at approximately one hundred dollars a month. However, his job entailed his absence at times. I think it had something to do with railroads which had most ill-advisedly then been put under temporary government control.

Elinor was intensely creative, and she did not seem to find herself lonely because there were one or two loyal women friends: just the prim, well-bred sort of creatures that one would never have expected to stay loyal, but perhaps their consciences were so unburdened and their sympathies so acute that they never thought to be anything but loyal among a raft of curiosity-seekers and insolent people who got a big kick out of cutting a lady they would once never have had an opportunity to know.

There was a burning hot summer when Horace and Elinor were too poor to leave town even for the comparatively inexpensive cottage in Somesville, and she stayed on, partly because his work kept him in Washington, and partly because she was writing continually. Her poems of that summer show a nostalgic desire for the cool black mountain streams of northern Maine, the blue lakes unexpectedly located near the top of mountains, the dark pines, the chill water-lilies, the long streams, and even the frosty breath of Mount Desert fogs.

Except for a short visit to attend my younger brother's wedding at Bar Harbor, she was penned in the sunny little house on Florida Avenue, which must have become almost a furnace during August. Any house in Washington is just that in August, particularly small thin-walled ones with a southern aspect.

Although she was very badly off in Washington for nearly three years, she did not seem unhappy, since my mother had given her a little house, a black fur coat and a black hat with greenish-blue feathers, which hat became her helmet, her token of victory. Elinor had always a tendency to duplicate things, so she bought another hat with her first check for a poem, and it was very nearly the same sort of helmet, except that the feathers were bluish-green instead of greenish-blue. In her collected verse there is a poem called "Green Hair," which I think was written more to these two hats than to any human being!

She came down to our house every afternoon, breasting the winter winds like Nikë, and had tea with us. There were many things disembodied about Elinor—toward the end of her life she grew almost impatient of food—but she did love

Washington, D. C.

THE SCHOOLGIRL OF FIFTEEN

things like hot toast, small scones, fresh asparagus and the first new potatoes to be found in market.

Under the stress of economy, she was vastly impressed by a market's advertisement in the newspaper which proclaimed the merits of "Frozen New Zealand Mutton." It was a situation which at the time made me feel almost weepy. To realize that Elinor, who always passed up the meat in favor of the more succulent and, it must be confessed, the most expensive new vegetable, went and bought a monstrous piece of "Frozen New Zealand Mutton" and spent several days trying to thaw it and trying to cook it! She was so accustomed to buying four double French chops from a rib of baby lamb that I consider it showed a good deal of courage to try to tackle this mummified sheep! As I said before, she was always a good cook, and we enjoyed almost as many meals prepared by her at the little Florida Avenue house as she shared with us in the big house.

Her meetings with other people, the first American equivalent to her own kind of people that she had met in seven years, took place in the sitting-room of our house, and anyone who met her once would go through snow and sleet to meet her again.

Horace and she became great friends with the three owners of Washington's high-brow book store, then in an experimental stage and now one of the very best book shops in the country. It was in a tiny room below the surface of H Street then. Now it is across the street at Seventeenth and H. But the same taste which started it still prevails.

61

Besides Sinclair Lewis and his wife, there was another old Yale college friend of my brother Henry who had met Elinor some years earlier when Henry brought him to Washington at the Easter vacation. His name was William Rose Benét, and in that chaotic post-war Washington he was editing a journal for the Department of Commerce and feeling very lonely. Sometimes he came to our house for Sunday lunch and sometimes we all had supper at Elinor's little house. She would read her poems, and although my brother Morton and I were severe, savage, raw and untutored, we were the first to hear her poems read aloud to Mr. Benét who proceeded to get some of them taken by New York high-brow weeklies. Bill was a very old friend of mine. I had known him since I was three and I expected him to be struck all of a heap by her verse. However, he was struck all of a heap by Elinor, although he did not confess as much for several months.

The first intimations of success began to come in. Verse, and even great poetry, is hardly remunerative, but there must be a certain thrill in finding that other people know just how good you are. I do not doubt for a moment that Mr. Lewis and Mr. Benét helped her by encouraging her.

At first Elinor did not dare run off to New York permanently. Instead she accepted the scattered invitations which came in after the publication of some of her recent work. But the first real recognition was an invitation to dinner at the Poetry Society, and I remember how excited we all were and how much she and I talked about what she should wear, for Elinor, who had always had the most beautiful French dresses, had had no use for formal evening dress in several years and was slightly put to it to decide. She showed little fear and not very much vanity, but it is in a way pathetic that she could not walk in and get a beautiful evening dress from one of the better shops. However, results were extremely successful. She found a seamstress who made up a classic white crêpe de Chine tunic tied with a gold cord around the waist. She wore gold leaves in her hair, and I expect she looked like a cross between Artemis and Athene. Unexpectedly, they asked her to make a speech, which terrified her and brought back a slight childish stutter left over from years before. Two days later she was back in Washington and said with reason that the occasion had been successful. There was even talk about bringing out a book of her verse. This was around February, 1921.

After the Poetry Society dinner and the exciting news of the decision of Harcourt, Brace and Howe to take the book of her new poetry, she worked almost all the time preparing the poems, choosing the title, reading us her latest pieces, and enjoying a glorious renaissance of creative ability. She commuted to New York for a few days every two weeks throughout another hot summer, and this was not quite so expensive as it might seem because she shared there a very small apartment with Miss Bernice Kenyon.

The New Republic, The Century, Poetry Magazine, Vanity Fair and other periodicals were accepting her poems, and she was adjusting herself to the complex demands of a highly difficult profession which has a certain amount of trying

63

commercial and business details connected with it. For poets must eat, editors have to be interviewed occasionally, and, although a writer's spirit may long for an aloof detached life, there are office boys to be pushed aside, snooty secretaries to be won over, and ideas which seem solid when thought over in the privacy of one's own room, nearly melt and dissolve under the searching stare of the editor.

Yet she managed to find a good deal of enjoyment and a great deal of valuable experience during these dog days in New York when she clung to subway straps or permitted herself the luxury of a Fifth Avenue bus. She was dressed in thin black crêpe, as mourning for her brother Henry, and she wrote me that, when she got back to the room which she and Miss Kenyon shared, her shoulders and slim body were stained as blue as fountain-pen ink.

This must have been the summer when she first met Edmund Wilson, then one of the editors of *Vanity Fair,* and John Dos Passos. They remained her intimate friends for the rest of her life. She would accept from "Bunny" Wilson the most severe criticisms which she would not have taken from anyone else. His slightly sour attitude toward life and letters appealed to her as a valuable astringent which she needed and wanted. Dos was the only son of a friend of Elinor's Great-Uncle Bill, who is something of a family hero, because of his Civil War record and the legend of his unfailing geniality. Apparently the father of Mr. Dos Passos was also a grand old man. They first came together because of this family feeling and later stayed friends in spite of any differences of opinion. Elinor was conservative, uninterested in modern sociological problems and, as she has stated in one of her more frivolous verses, "A Member of the Primrose League," and Dos is, I believe, what we used to call years ago a "Radical."

She was not then in that highly organized circle which composes the cream of New York literary society. Log-rolling, I think, always confused her even after she became a person who was obliged to attend literary teas. Horace and she wrote to each other every day. She was in the habit of sending manuscript poems to him in her letters, and she frequently sent them also to my mother and even to me. We had for so long constituted her audience that the habit kept on, and she never quite outgrew it, for she read aloud parts of all of her books to us from the manuscript whenever we were together.

CHAPTER

❖ 8 ❖

Two exciting things happened that winter. With the perspective of time it seems ridiculous to compare them, but in November, 1921, we did. Elinor's first published book of verse appeared under the Harcourt imprint, and I "came out" in the middle of the Washington Conference.

Nets to Catch the Wind was a little, light brown book, which Elinor complained looked slightly like a primer on elemental geometry. It was not unattractive, but its format was hardly inspiring. Still, I think it amused her later on to have had that first book published with a binding not unlike *The New England Primer,* and she always felt deeply grateful to Harcourt, Brace and Howe for publishing it. The critical acclaim which it received startled Elinor more than it did the rest of us. I think she was in many ways modest, although she knew exactly the value of her own work. What surprised her was that other people were so kind as to find in it excellence.

As for the second event of importance—to get this now so unimportant event over quickly, it was a small dance, the first

66

given in thirteen years by any member of my close family in Washington, and, to my great astonishment, it was a vast success, only marred by the fact that Elinor *would* not come to it. She stayed in New York in case her presence should antagonize the parents of a few young people. She would not appear for fear of jeopardizing my popularity. Of course, the party seemed incomplete without her. At the next one we insisted on her presence, and it was extremely amusing for all of us to have her there looking about twenty years old and, in many ways, younger than I.

My mother gave me that second dinner and dance in February, 1922. It was called the "Black and White Party," a way of achieving fancy dress without forcing too much expenditure on young friends not particularly affluent. Elinor was squired by John Peale Bishop, a solid young Princetonian, then an editor of *Vanity Fair,* I think, and I know he was co-author with "Bunny" Wilson of several books, particularly *The Undertaker's Garland.* Horace was away working on the railroads and had been all the way out to the West Coast. So Elinor was temporarily just a very pretty young woman. She had on black and silver with a coronet of shiny patent-leather leaves in her hair, which sounds hideous but, in fact, did actually make her look like a slightly mournful bacchante. Johnny Bishop, who was staying at a club, put on the most amazing eighteenth-century costume with ruffles and wore a peruke powdered and tied with a black ribbon; this magnificence kept dinner waiting a full hour, but none of us minded. We had enticed my mother into a sleek black "transformation," and I was wearing an entire wig of white curls. Most of the boys had on simple variations of the dinner-jacket, and the girls had each been able to confect something amusing with either a black or a white dance frock. We beguiled the hour while John kept us waiting with rather mild cocktails and a great many jokes.

Elinor had as good a time as my contemporaries or I and seemed full of gaiety and high spirits. Later on at the dance a rather fatuous but admiring old cotillion leader, the only cotillion leader in Washington and an amiable if silly character, asked me repeatedly the name and the age of my little "school-girl sister." It is an exact fact that "my little school-girl sister" was Elinor. She was, you can gather, having a good time, and she was enjoying almost more the fact that I was having a good time.

This was the only one of my *fêtes* in Washington she would ever attend, and it is always a source of pleasure to remember what fun we all had and how informal the whole thing was. I do not think young people hold the rancors of their parents deliberately. Although these were not high-brow young persons and may not have been appreciative as yet of her work, they were glad to have her with them, and she felt it. But her life was to be more and more set into the groove of a hard-working writer, a writer with some genius as well as much application, and she never returned again for what General Washington calls, in his letters, "a pretty little frisk," although she did come back to visit us now and again.

As the demands of her writing grew she severed most of

68

the threads holding her to Washington. Horace was away a good deal of the time and no doubt she put much of her enthusiasm for home-making into creative work. Creative work is a curious thing which distracts the mind and body with its insistent demands, like a gadfly or bumblebee that cannot be driven away. She could not know that she had only seven more years of life ahead of her, but she did seem to feel that the pent-up longing to write, held back for ten years, was now a freshet which could not be dammed. About the time of her delightful visit to Washington for the Black and White Party, she determined to take a room where she might be alone with her typewriter.

New York changes all the time, but Washington Square North remains pretty much the way it has always been. Elinor found a large, high-ceilinged room on the entrance floor of 1, University Place which was then still one of the great old houses facing the Square. And this she turned into her own sort of sanctuary, a room in which she lived and worked, and in the bathroom she even cooked, but no trace of these mundane activities was visible. That one room looked like a mixture of Horace Walpole, Lady Mary Wortley Montague and Miss Austen. I can't imagine where she slept in it, but I can remember that all her dressing-table equipment was neatly encased in a cupboard in the bathroom, and a tiny outfit for cooking was also stowed away there with almost mathematical precision. In the dusk of early spring the lamps and candles glowed under the high ceiling of a drawing-room which would have been suitable as one of a lady's twenty

rooms but seemed slightly ridiculous and almost unbelievable as the only dwelling-place of a human being. Yet at 1,
University Place were spent her gayest and most frivolous
months. She was making deep friendships and dozens of
casual acquaintanceships. Benét, Wilson, Dos Passos, Bishop
and several others were often dropping in with their wives or
best girls or just by themselves to take her out to dinner. She
had not started prose writing and the practice of poetry was
not very profitable, but there was Marta's crowded little restaurant off Washington Square for ordinary evenings, the
Lafayette Hotel for more elegant binges, and apartments
around that part of town where people could talk till all
hours, apartments owned by people like Coby Gilman and
Mr. and Mrs. Herbert Gorman, and almost more home-like
than her own eighteenth-century nest at 1, University Place.

Occasionally she and her newest beau, Bill Benét, would
meet Sinclair Lewis of an evening, and he would persuade
her, for her own benefit and the amusement of others, toward prose, a more lucrative employment. And so, in 1,
University Place, she began writing that strictly stylized
satire, *Jennifer Lorn.* In the meantime, she was busy pouring
out poetry and was happy to realize that *Vanity Fair* would
employ her in a few months as poetry editor at the vast sal-
ary of fifty dollars a week.

She began to care more intensely for clothes—not that she
had ever ceased to care for them, but the tempting windows
of New York and the great variety of fascinating garments
offered made her selections more and more perfect. It is not

usual to find a woman writer of great talent always soignée and perfectly dressed. Some people even seemed to feel critical of Elinor's curled hair, her coral-colored finger nails and her slim ankles. But, personally, I should think that they would have seen in her vanity, if it were that, a striving toward the same perfection she reached in writing.

She was very apt at this time to use a ballad form. No matter how annoying the ballad form or its emotional contents and phraseology might seem to the observer, Elinor had good reason to use it. Her nurse through many years of childhood had been a cranky, picturesque old Scotch-Irish woman from a part of Ulster called Balli-something or other, and Elinor had imbibed ballads before she could write them, when Mary Anne MacDonald sang to her interminable unwritten sagas. "The Prinkin' Leddie" would seem artificial, except that she knew modern Scotch-Irish, not by written word, but by heart and by ear.

When she was traveling she scribbled her verse on lined scratch pads, although later she carried out her fondness for perfection to a point where she used only the most delicate blue bond paper for typewriting and a bluish-green typewriter ribbon. These first poems which came home from her occasional visits away or from her fastness at 1, University Place, were "Incantation" and the poem to me called "Nancy," in her handwriting; "The Tortoise in Eternity," rather badly typed; "The Eagle and the Mole," not typed very well; a sonnet called "Ivory Statuette," which I have not seen published; and there must have been many others in rough draft,

71

but these are the ones I have under my hand at the moment.

Back in 1919, my brother Henry, who was Elinor's nearest contemporary in the family, had slightly irritated us by telling her that she ought to meet a *real* poet, as we thought she had the makings of a real poet, if she were not already one herself. We thought his choice of words unhappy, but two or three years later he was to be proved right, for the real poet that he wanted her to meet turned out to be Miss Edna St. Vincent Millay. By 1921 and 1922 all of young America interested in beautiful letters and beautiful poetry was aware of her and very admiring. When Elinor met Edna, they immediately liked each other, and it was a somehow beautiful and inspiring sight to see these two, each so lovely, outwardly and physically, becoming the warmest sort of friends, completely cognizant each of the other's merit, quite above petty jealousies or irritations, and still further above minor irritations.

The small and lovely Edna had been much admired by my younger brother and myself for two years. We loved *A Few Figs from Thistles, Renascence* and *Second April.* We had read avidly her more frivolous pieces which had appeared in *Vanity Fair* and other magazines and finally in book form under the pseudonym of Nancy Boyd. When Miss Millay as Miss Boyd chose to be humorous and brilliantly witty she, by some miracle, escaped being bitter or rancorous. Her recognition came before Elinor's, but she was as friendly and admiring on the day she met my sister as on that sad afternoon when she said a last few words to a dead friend. They made

72

a very striking appearance together, although you did not feel that appearance was a major interest with them—the one so tall, so like a falcon, pink and white and chestnut, and the other, tiny, subtly exquisite, cream and red-gold. I do not think it is usual for two exquisite women of equal or rival talents to become great friends. It is a tribute to them to record that they did.

Elinor had a blithe way of skipping what might seem intolerable difficulties to other people. Once when I felt the noose of marriage growing very tight around my silly throat, and showed twenty-year-old despair about it, she took one look at my terrified face—I was cowering in the bathroom, which I considered the only sanctuary left in the house where I could hide, for the other rooms seemed piled, to me, with wedding presents, a veil, a dress of white satin, boxes of cake and congratulatory letters—and she rescued me with an understanding smile. She said, "Why get married if you don't want to?" It sounds as simple as the Lady from Philadelphia, but at the time it was a miracle of comprehension for which I was deeply grateful. Her prophecies came true. I was much happier, not obliged to get married, and the young man in question has admitted since then that he also was much happier. We have become fast friends. Elinor did not seem angry, whereas everybody else, except my younger brother, looked on me for a few days with mingled curiosity and horror. She said blithely that the proposed wedding had given her a good excuse to buy a new dress and that I was, please, to keep the earrings she had given me as a

73

wedding gift! . . . Not that Elinor was in the habit of breaking up young romances. She was incurably addicted to helping them along. I have never known her to be anything but friendly toward any form of young love, successful or blackly disappointed.

She liked jokes, did not object to teasing, could stand verbal and written attacks without loss of her smile or her equanimity. She urged me to do a caricature of her in one of my so unimportant novels, and when *The New Yorker* was searching for a portrait of her, she wrote one with an adroit humor which was not entirely compassionate toward her own frailties. She was not a glass figure easily knocked off a mantelpiece, but it is true that with her best friends she avoided vituperation and was not much given to cruel forms of teasing or practical jokes, although she did accept them from others. Occasionally that slight sense of injustice which must attack all of us at times would make her remark a little plaintively, "But I really *was* in mourning, and even if she does say black was an affectation, she would have hopped on me harder if I had worn colors!" But even savage satire directed against her would draw from her only a slightly rueful grin.

It was a great excitement, but a controlled, carefully guarded secret when she began to be occupied with the idea of writing *Jennifer Lorn.* This, her first novel, did not seem to interrupt her poetry, but at the start she did not expect it to please people very much, and was extremely thrilled and surprised to find that George Doran was disposed to publish

74

it. She planned that spring (1923) to go to Mrs. MacDowell's Colony in New Hampshire and put in the hardest sort of work to make the book the required length and still longer for George Doran, that urbane and kindly man, who was one of her intimate friends.

I think she was also planning secretly to marry Bill Benét as soon as possible, because when I gave a great gasp of relief at escaping from marriage, she gave me an oblique look and said, "But people can't be *celibate!*" which was ridiculous as there was little danger for either of us.

Elinor could be secretive; mystery and intrigue in the strict sense of a hidden thing amused her. She would make a secret of a new hat and suddenly startle you with it. Or she would make a plan, sometimes unimportant, down to its most minute details and sparkle with delight at how well she had hidden it from you up to the last moment. At times she was infantile and transparent and sulky, but she could arrange schemes as delicately far-fetched and as artificial as a towering wedding cake, and she kept some of these castles carefully concealed. Horace and she had been brilliantly sly together, getting away from things and people that bored them. Now she was about to pop another surprise on all of us. She stayed friends with Horace, exchanged letters with him (she continued to do this until her death), and always had a proprietary feeling about him—*vide* "Once When My Husband Was a Child" from *Nets to Catch the Wind.* He was Horace and, when it pleased her, partly Gerald Poynyard or the protagonist of a poem. But she did get a divorce and she

75

did marry Bill Benét. And she stayed friends with Horace.

Almost everyone who knows Bill likes him. I had known him since my fourth year and certainly I liked him, but certainly also I was a little bit astonished.

Elinor was married to Bill at the apartment of a friend. Esther Root, who afterward became Mrs. F. P. A., was her maid of honor, and F. P. A. held Bill's hand, metaphorically speaking. He was Bill's best man, I suppose. She had orchids from Mr. Untermeyer's hothouse and good wishes from all of us, but she did not ask us to the ceremony. It was more fun without us.

Bill and Elinor were very happy and extremely kind toward first stumbling efforts of mine. I had just managed to get two stories taken by Mencken and Nathan for the *Smart Set,* soon to cease but then my goal. Bill cut out and sent me my first "puff," a notice by Burton Rascoe. Elinor continuously praised me and encouraged me at such exciting places as the Algonquin at lunch time, which was my idea of heaven when I could get to New York for a day or two in 1923. Bill and Elinor took me to friends' like Carl Van Vechten's, where there were people like Carl and Fania, and things like cats and pictures and books and drinks and cigarettes of such superb quality and elegance that a person of slightly less than twenty-one was honored extremely by an invitation. It was a great deal of fun going around with them. Elinor had already a special group of fans—Carl was one of them. She was working hard and was going to a fair amount of parties, but there was not yet the pressure of engagements and telephones, of contracts and promises, which demanded so much of her later on. They lived near Gramercy Square, I think partly because she had undertaken the care of Bill's three children and they went to school near by. It was rather a large undertaking for a writer, not at all strong herself, but she seemed to like having a big family of big children.

Elinor always had favorites, favorite people and favorite things; she would even have favorite colors for taxis and make one wait for ages on a street corner until the right kind came along. She had a favorite among Bill's three children, the youngest girl whom she adored, and this little girl came down with diphtheria. Elinor nursed her devotedly for weeks, including the long weakness of convalescence which was perhaps harder, for there was no elevator in the building and Elinor toted the little girl up several flights of stairs after her first airings in Gramercy Park. She invented stories for her, and Bill drew pictures to while away the invalid's siege.

They must have been nice stories, for I can remember the ones she made up for me when I was five and six. These were a collection, a sort of saga about two or three little girls who were not allowed to have any ice-cream except plain vanilla, or any gay dresses or funny papers on Sunday, because such things weren't "nice." So a huge baby, a good fairy but as big as a bear, called the "giant child," a fat, jolly, blond object in blue rompers, came along every evening just after they went to bed and beguiled their dull lives. He hid chocolate peppermints as big as plates under their pillows, he produced toys from capacious blue linen pockets, and he

77

was a jovial chuckling companion as soon as their ferocious governess withdrew. Elinor never wrote any children's stories, but she could invent wonderful ones. I suppose it was the same imagination that made it possible for her to write about another century and be at home in it, not grimly or pedantically, but with gay detail.

It seems to me that I have omitted entirely mentioning one small apartment they were in for a few months. It must have been when they were in New York not long after they were married. It was in Greenwich Village near Sheridan Square on a short, sunny, rather messy side street. That was when the Village was *really* the village—oh, foolish remark always made by sentimental retrospecters like me! Because, of course, when the village was really the village depends entirely on one's own age, state of emotion and rude health. For all I know modern young people who now live below Fourteenth Street will be looking back in ten years' time to 1934 and using just the same italics.

At any rate, it was a tiny, cheerful apartment, a walk-up and rather cramped, but we had a wonderful time. I was chastely domiciled for a few days in the Junior League Club, miles uptown, and never went near it for twenty of the twenty-four hours. I recall one afternoon when Elinor and I went out shopping in wop shops for interesting hors d'oeuvres, artichoke hearts, olives, thin slices of salami and segments of cheese. We each had on one of her wash-silk dresses, for it was a very warm Indian summer. On her feet were greeny-blue Morocco slippers, and on mine a pair of too-big gold kid dance sandals, because my new Junior Leaguish shoes pinched and I had left them upstairs. No one seemed to find us a strange or sorry spectacle as we dawdled home about six o'clock with our arms full of packages. The entire population of that street was Italian, except for the people in the converted house where Bill and she were living, and the Italians were not disturbed apparently by odd footwear or hatless women.

After such an afternoon Bill would bring back some drink, Rosemary and Steve Benét would come around, and we would descend on Marta's for a huge dinner in the garden. One night a most attractive young man from Oxford came along with us. He was very good-looking and he was going to be a writer. After all of us had talked shop for hours back at the little flat he offered to take me home to the League Club house in his car. The next day I bleated for hours to Elinor. "Sixty-three blocks I rode with Jack and he never made one pass at me! Sixty-three whole blocks without making a pass! I must be a leper."

Another night we ended up at Herbert Gorman's, where there was a young painter who had made a splendid painting of "Red" Lewis and another of Dorothy Parker. He had a police dog that I fed dreamily with crisp Swedish bread, which it seemed to relish, while I nearly went to sleep from glorious fatigue and could just dimly hear Elinor and Jean and Herbert and Wolf and Bill talking in what sounded like an agreeable murmur. These friends were kind to me because I was Elinor's sister and comparatively unannoying at that

79

time. If we were very late at such a party there was always room on a sofa for me, or Bill would nobly donate his bed. He was reputed to be a great grouch in the early morning before he went to work at *The Saturday Review,* but I never noticed it. It was a family joke, his grouchiness, which I rather doubt. Anyway, I slept solidly until midday.

This was the jazz era when the Village was *really* . . . you know what I mean.

Then, on another visit that autumn, I treated Elinor and Bill to a night in a suite at the Algonquin which seemed to me a very desirable spot. There was a boy I knew who was coming down with typhoid—but I did not know that—and Donald Ogden Stewart who was funnier than I ever heard anyone and appreciated by us all. Elinor sat on my bed until four in the morning talking nonsense, for which I cursed her because it spoiled my night's sleep and interrupted my private monologue about the charms of a young publisher who spurned my affections. She was always quite a person for talking the night away, and that night she was very brilliant until I forced her to go and join William and leave me to dreams.

She did not seem very much older than I was just at this time. It was much more like seven years than seventeen, the gap between us, if it was that.

I would go back to Washington with my arms full of Elinor's books and a spotted Spark Plug, the toy race-hoss presented by Bill. That was a good time, that was.

It seems necessary to say, in contradiction to one of her

TAKEN IN WAR-TIME ENGLAND, 1916. ELINOR HAD JUST GROWN HER HAIR
AFTER HER FIRST "BOB" AND WAS EXPERIMENTING WITH BANGS—

friends and commentators, that Elinor's actions were not particularly "semi-public," as he states, nor was her life anything but private and secret. Her *tastes,* on the other hand, were pretty well known even by those who did not know her, and they were comparatively unchangeable, from the Wedgwood lamps and eighteenth-century furniture which decorated her living quarters, to the long shelves about Shelley or anything that might have interested Shelley, which guarded her walls.

If she took liberties with Shelley it was because one may take liberties with a semi-sacred creature, who has been the object of one's passion for years. She even liked to be kidded about him by ignoramuses such as myself. What joy was hers when she met a fellow enthusiast!

While at *Vanity Fair* her only vacation was at the Mac-Dowell Colony in New Hampshire which she loved although she made fun of it. She always showed both affection and gratitude toward Mrs. MacDowell and the Colony, even when she described to me (who ever hated the rustic scene) the early breakfasts, the long days spent in the small cabins where one was supposed to be creative and obliged to be lonely, for rules were very strict against visiting between cabins, the lunch of milk and sandwiches, silently left on the doorstep, and, later on, the evenings when a group of geniuses were supposed to chat together about their impulses toward work during the day but, instead, behaved very much as you and I might, were we getting together in a homogeneous group of varying mores every evening after eight or nine

81

hours of solitude. It is not quite so easy to turn the tap of genius off or on, and I fancy there were moments in those scattered cabins when all the mature creative artists were just so many rebellious kindergarten children, forced into temporary solitary confinement, as if it were a punishment. But Elinor was deeply grateful for the enforced working, perhaps because she was never lazy and made of her work almost a fetish and a luxury. She felt that here at least she was not being cruel or wicked if she spent hours working, but was indeed complying with the rules as much as any boarding-school child could. Not only was she grateful to Mrs. Mac-Dowell and the founders of the Colony, but she felt an affection for the place which was to my undisciplined self rather hard to understand. To get up early in the morning and go to a small cabin about one-eighth of a mile away from any other human soul, and to be obliged to stay there until the long shadows of sunset descended, seemed to me a good deal like putting a heavy check-rein and a bridle upon Pegasus, but Elinor claimed to like it, and the Colony certainly helped her finish two of her books, as it must have helped other people in their creative work. She would permit herself an occasional joke about this enforced regimentation which smacks a little of Girl Scouts, but never would she say anything unkind or disagreeable about a place which does, in effect, give to so many people who write and compose and paint, the fresh air that they need so much. There are times when certain temperaments cannot stand the garret, even with white hyacinths included, and the pine woods of New

Hampshire give them the needed change and repose. To Elinor, Peterborough was a sort of celestial typewriter, and since she was always happy when she was quite alone, unless she was very ill, she was almost always happy there. For there she was almost always alone.

CHAPTER

❖ 9 ❖

JENNIFER LORN had an attractive format, very eighteenth-century, with a nice little engraving and satisfying type. It was a pleasant book to look at and touch. The contents pleased the discriminating and pleased a good many non-high-brows, too, who naturally feel just as discriminating as others that have greater justification. Its author loved the fact that it was a pretty thing to have around. It was one of her few books which I never heard at all in bits and pieces before publication. She had turned to fiction partly to earn more money, indeed largely for that reason, but the success of *Jennifer* was a delight. She met so many people who became her great friends through *Jennifer*—Emily Clark and Mr. Cabell and lots of others.

It does not date or age, partly because it is a period "conversation piece." It re-reads well and is quite free of what my cynical grandmother would call the "Prithee-me-lord" touch. I have no excuse or right to make any critical valuations because, in spite of seven months of book reviewing, my critical

84

faculty is undisciplined and undeveloped, but I do wish that Elinor had curtailed *Jennifer* to exclude most of the Persian part. Any number of times I've heard people say that they liked that part best, but my prejudice continues. It seems to me that the limber steel of the first two-thirds of the book gets tarnished by the rosewater, the saffron and vanilla essence and pistachio nuts of the last chapters. The rest is damascened, supple and even fragile, but it is veritable steel, and I don't think the book needed the part before the end. It seems to me that one swift rub, a quick polish and ending would have kept her blade bright. Perhaps she meant to be ironic about her princely pastry-cook, to wash her rapier in soft scented water and leave the steel to rust. She was seldom inadvertent.

When *Black Armour,* her second book of verse, appeared in 1923, many of the poems had already come out in magazines. A great many times they were so good that one couldn't help clipping them to keep, but it was fine to have them all together, and again the format was attractive. She had luck in that always. Her books were invariably good-looking. *Black Armour* had a silver and black jacket, one of the first silver paper wrappers I ever saw. She was widely known as a poet by this time. The audience in America who read and buy poets' work now recognized her. *Jennifer* was coming out in England, and she was thinking of another novel because, no matter how well received the poems were, or how well placed in a magazine, they were hardly money-makers. Indeed, short poems never net very much in checks from the magazine printing them. The only exception to this in Elinor's case which I can remember was a long Christmas ballad which she was commissioned to cable from London to a woman's magazine with a huge circulation in America. She was paid at so much a word and asked to make it a certain length and to cable it with all punctuation very carefully. As this order came during the hot thunder showers of a sultry July week-end and as the time limit was very short, she was not particularly grateful but groaned and swore at having to invent anything so unseasonable against her secret judgment. Such writing did not please her, while the spontaneous bursts of either serious poetry or cheerful scraps made up for her own edification and the amusement of friends would come from her mind to her typewriter, or her lips, and put her into a gay mood for the rest of the day.

After the winter in the Gramercy Square apartment, Elinor became enamored of a cottage at New Canaan. It was quite old and I suppose the spring was quite new when she first saw it, that time of year when lilacs and new leaves make almost any pretty Connecticut dwelling house of sufficient years and charm irresistible to the impressionable city-dweller's eye. She saw it, she liked it, Bill liked it, they were sentimental about New Canaan because they had spent a week's honeymoon there, and they quickly convinced each other that it would be splendid for his three children and her work. They had several friends in New Canaan and there were schools. Elinor had inherited enough of the lawyer from her father to sum up a perfect brief in favor of anything she

86

very much approved of at the time. The New Canaan house probably was very attractive in springtime, but I should have thought she would consider about that hour or so from New York. But she went ahead and bought it on one of those so cheery-looking arrangements with most of the purchase remaining on the mortgage. From that summer on the mortgage rang through her letters to her family and friends and even intruded into letters to a friendly editor, Carl Van Doren. It was always good for a desperate groan from Elinor; and then she would start a conversation and soon forget it entirely. It was a whipping boy and an alibi, that mortgage.

They all moved to New Canaan, taking a German maid who, for an immense wage, did a still more immense amount of work, partly because she was allowed to keep her dachshund. Bill had to get up at dawn to catch a train for his office, and Elinor rose at almost the same time to get the children off to school. She fussed a good deal about the furnishings and a good deal about food, for she was on a diet and naturally the others were all pretty hungry living in the country and walking a mile from school or station before their supper.

She was again wracked by violent headaches, which she found were due to abnormally high blood pressure, pressure dangerously high for anyone, and hardly credible for a woman of her age. She worried herself by bothering a great deal about details, by working very hard in the morning after skipping breakfast, and by thinking about the mortgage or the recalcitrant furnace. Of course, it soon became bitter

87

cold; her excursions to town were somewhat limited by conditions; and there were all the usual domestic troubles of a newly acquired house, complicated by the obvious fact that if your only servant is one highly paid, invaluable person and she gets sick, you are in the soup and must prepare the meals and stoke the furnace yourself. Elinor, goaded by high blood pressure and her own nature, forced herself, with a bitter half-pleasure, to do ridiculous things sometimes which over-taxed her. She must have missed the telephone calls of New York even though she liked her neighbors. It is not too easy to hustle into an old fur coat and rush for the last commuter's special after the theater when one has been used to first nights, shining evening wraps and taxis, followed by talk and parties which lasted well into the night.

I wonder sometimes that New Canaan lasted as long as it did, for it was not convenient for Bill, and Elinor had to take refuge at the Peterborough Colony in order to finish up any urgent work. Luckily someone else liked the look of the cottage which she had fixed up very attractively, and it finally found a purchaser.

It was during that cold winter that she gave a few lectures, one far afield in Chicago and two nearer home. I gathered from her shudders and extremely brief descriptions that she really loathed lecturing and could not have kept on. Usually her return from any new experience, a literary meeting, public or private, any Book Fair or party or office-tea, would bring vivid descriptions and lively personal reactions even if she emphatically insisted on hating something or some person connected with the foray; but lecturing returned her to us silent and unhappy.

We were alarmed about her health, and a favorite doctor gave her quite serious warnings about diet and strain and over-exertion. She paid some attention at last. The three Benét children went off with their aunt, Kathleen Norris, Bill's first wife's sister. This best-selling aunt had taken them with her to California before; she was devoted to them, gave them the most delightful time imaginable in her big house out there, and was in every way a second mother and a generous godmother. (I saw a newspaper picture of her this year with both girls, now grown-up young ladies. All three were festooned with orchids, but I think I knew at once the one Elinor had been particularly fond of because she still fitted the ecstatic description given me ten years ago of a little girl. Elinor loved the other child, too, and kept saying how good she was to everyone, and what a sweet disposition she had. Perhaps she felt a little bit guilty at having a favorite. In the photograph both seemed equally pretty now, and Mrs. Norris looked very proud of them.)

The house on West Ninth Street, it seems to me, *is* Elinor at the time of her novels and poems. It was a pleasant time for nearly everyone of us. No matter how often I am told in angry editorials and brilliant articles by leading economists of the evils of the years 1925-1928, that these years were mad, bad and dangerous to know, I will never supinely agree that the prosperous times were a wicked mania and that the five years of depression have been more normal and healthy.

89

Those years were fun, at least. Writers and painters and their overlords, the publishers and galleries and their underlings, the loquacious visiting colored maids and philosophic taxi-drivers were all happy and fairly satisfied. Not many of us were bloated with lucre, but it was nice to take taxis and eat what you liked, so the money we made circulated quickly or, to use a typical expression of the time, "got around a lot." Today, if the employer can barely afford a bus, it means that the maid may have to walk a good many blocks to work and then find an empty ice-box on arrival. In the much criticized fat years what wonders met the eye even in modest refrigerators! They were like campaign slogans.

Ninth Street, just west of Fifth Avenue, is a very pleasing street. I rarely look down it any longer because it makes me sad to remember that even if I leapt from the bus and tore down the sidewalk and rushed up the steps and pressed the bell under Bill's neat lettering of the names BENÉT WYLIE (always two names below Twelfth Street if both partners worked), no answering click would greet me. I would see the names on the card only in a dream, and in dreams one never hears satisfactory real sounds like the click of a front door.

It was a big flat taking up the whole second floor of a fair-sized brownstone, which had not been changed very much in sixty years, although it was well kept up. The front room was the formal sitting-room and dining-room, with a little study off it crowded with Bill's books and pictures. White shelves of books, gay and leather-bound—some very fine

90

and some just readable, or beloved, or interesting—lined two walls. There were high windows onto Ninth Street. The blue velveteen sofa, not yet really shabby, the Wedgwood lamp, the eighteenth-century silver mirror, the tables, the beautifully shaped chairs, the fruit-and-flower picture over the fireplace, new chairs that were only new in the sense that they were recent acquisitions, grand reading lights and a frivolous china lady and gentleman of Chelsea on the mantelpiece,—they were all Elinor. It was not too big a room to seem quite small and cozy when pleasantly filled with intimates. Back of this was a little passage, a bathroom which Bill and I or any friend was allowed to use (Elinor grew so fussy about her own that she would never let us go into it or rumple one of her hand towels), and then a pretty double bedroom which her passion for formality of appearance had made her arrange in such a way that it looked more like a small parlor furnished in maple where two maple beds with ducks'-egg-blue chintz petticoats had somehow strayed. She had a little powdering table of smooth applewood with a patina of age. Inside were a looking-glass and powder, scent and semi-precious jewelry in neat compartments: nothing was ever disarranged. If she ever scattered powder in these later years it must have been secretly. In her semi-sacred bathroom where we rude yokels were not supposed to penetrate, all was spotless and tidy; even the creams and lotions and little box of pale rouge (yes, pale rouge, not violently red) never seemed to be disarranged, and the lids were never left off them.

91

Separated from the bedroom by two open arches on either side of a fireplace was the back room where she worked on an enormous deal table unpainted and unvarnished. There were two high windows facing south, usually open, and one whole wall was covered with books on shelves, all the books she loved to work with, Americana and everything about Shelley, rows of shabby old books on subjects that interested her, collections made in the idea that sometime she might write her "witch book" (of which more later), travels and little-known volumes on old explorations and outmoded early nineteenth-century guides to the Grand Tour.

Above the fireplace were flower prints bought before they were the fashion, and a valentine of great charm sent by William on the last fourteenth of February. There was a comfortable chair and a delicate, uncomfortable chaise-longue she used herself. Her typing paper was greenish-blue and so were her pencils. She had a Chinese porcelain bowl with a mulberry-pink lining for erasers and clips. The table was loaded with papers and books and work in progress, but all were arranged in mathematical precision. Next the table was a door into a nice human little kitchen, and a small cheerful, sunny room, obviously intended for a dining-room, but never in three years used for anything but the dumping of unwanted books and discarded wrapping paper.

It was a nice apartment, lived in, worked in, played in, and it had Elinor's own aloof charm. It did not look half so hard-working as it was. It managed to appear leisurely and unruffled.

There had been friends in the University Place days, but now there were more. With few exceptions the people she had known there were still intimates. She had, it was true, less of an intimacy with a certain lady poet, a real patron of the arts but unfortunately also very patronizing to artists; and quite often she had nine-day feuds with some individual, but the feuds did not often last even that long. In fact, her quick recoveries were disconcerting to a degree. After you had agreed that So-and-So was a repulsive friend with malicious intention, it was only too likely that the following week So-and-So would telephone, and they would talk about some new book with complete accord, and usually Elinor would ask So-and-So to Sunday night supper.

She had loved going to Richmond, and Emily Clark was a friend she never quarreled with. A good many people lived down near Elinor, and others came downtown and asked her in return to their own haunts. These invitations produced typical Elinor groans because of the length of the drive or the cost of the taxi, but she usually accepted, and Bill and she would be out until very late.

There was Ernest Boyd, sardonic and brown and aristocratic, laughing and doing jokes in a low Dublin accent, and Madeleine, talking rapidly a mixture of French and English and telling all the gossip in New York, while she wandered around the bedroom like a plump partridge with improbably tiny feet in pretty slippers and followed Elinor to the sacred powder table or still more sacred make-up cabinet above the washstand. There was a semi-sour badinage between Mon-

93

sieur and Madame B—— which was extremely diverting for the uninvolved listener. Carl Van Doren sat on a sofa and admitted he made the best oatmeal in the world. Bunny Wilson would not come if anyone else was there, but would talk half the night to Elinor long after Bill had retired, giving her writing a savage criticism which she accepted from no one else. Dorothy Parker, vivid, sympathetic and never showing the caustic side which is in many of her poems and stories, would spend the afternoon in the back room between the table with the typewriter and the book-shelves, a place where few penetrated. Elinor loved Dorothy, and they liked having some of the same hates. Mrs. Parker, looking very tiny, with enormous dark eyes as big as the dog's in Hans Andersen's story, would get up from the uncomfortable chaise-longue and rush out for a dinner date. She almost never stayed for dinner because she always had a new best beau. Marc Connelly, then the least intimidating of all the high-brows to a raw interloper like myself, dropped in of an evening. He would make everyone weak with laughter, unless he forced us to do some terrible brain-teasing parlor game of his own invention in which he shone, while the rest of us racked our silly heads. There were Steve Benét and Rosemary, who was very close to Elinor and one of her favorites. The Gormans came in a lot. Bill and Elinor shared the magnificent Marjorie with them. She worked for the Gormans in the forenoon and the Benéts in the afternoon, and sandwiched in a music lesson somewhere, for she had an operatic voice which was really good. Edna Millay and her husband, Eugen

94

Boissevain, spent the evening there when they were in New York and asked Elinor up to their farm which she liked immensely.

These and others I can remember well under the lamp in the sitting-room on Ninth Street. And going out to parties at Philip Moeller's or singing songs at Sigmund Spaeth's, or climbing up to a studio and finding drinks and books and pictures. It made a sort of small-town life, extraordinarily pleasant and intimate with gossip or sudden excitements ("Oh, Whooziz is going to do a book on the same subject. How awful; people will think I copied him, et-cetera"), but no smaller town than New York could have provided so many people with the same interests and amusements.

There were, of course, visiting firemen too. Although I never saw the Huxleys, I heard her descriptions and can remember that Aldous clocked in at every mention in the nearest time to Percy Bysshe Shelley. There was, of course, a fixed and immutable gulf between her most casual words about Shelley and whatever she might say about any other human being, ordinary or extraordinary, but Mr. Huxley stood alone for quite a while. I thought this rather difficult to bear because I was the Huxley fan at first. Elinor gave me *Leda* in 1919, and I was wild about *Limbo* in 1921. Both Mr. and Mrs. Huxley sounded very nice. She was, Elinor said, attractive—"like cherries, dark red ones almost black, with a lot of taste,"—and he was "a sort of angel."

Rebecca West she met when Miss West first came over to America. We had read her articles in *The New Republic*.

What was she like? I asked. Oh, very good-looking, not very English-looking because she didn't have that stem to her nose which most English people have (Miss West is Irish, we found out later on), very witty and s-s-sh . . . she had said some woman was a bitch! A few years later we all said it quite frequently, but at that time what a daring word it seemed!

And there was a very opinionated little Italian nobleman who was an orchestra leader with a beautiful wife (but that was later and I must try not to mix things up).

It was the visiting firemen who made Elinor want to go back to Europe again, the visitors and books and memories. She had been home nine years and was growing a little restive for a sight of her other country, England.

I had been over three times since the war, twice to England and once to France, and was always going around in Washington with those I called rudely, but with deep affection, "The Limeys," meaning the bachelors of H. B. M.'s Embassy. In the fall of 1925 I came back to America with half a novel under my arm, a childish and extremely cheerful story called *Roundabout,* which I was trying to finish in Washington.

Bill and Elinor were very good about it and would listen to large portions read aloud every time I came up to New York. It was about street fairs in Paris and their far-reaching results. I thought it very sophisticated, and Elinor liked its ingenuous gusto and never was so cattish as to call it ingenuous. She was invariably kind and constructive about my

96

work—I have never known her to be impatient or bored, and she was equally good to other writers. So many authors are too preoccupied with their own work to have any time for others'. My sister was never like that. A sympathetic ear can help a lot if it is also highly trained and fastidious. She was much more patient about one's work than about little things like being late or forgetting a telephone call; they would irritate her immensely.

I knew Mencken and idolized him, but had never met the Knopfs who were friends of Elinor's, although not that year her publishers. Doran had brought out *The Venetian Glass Nephew*.

Elinor knew that Bobbs-Merrill had turned my novel down and that I was in despair. A friend suggested letting Mencken read it. I hated to bother him with it, but of course I did, and when he wrote and said he liked it and thought I should show it to Alfred and Blanche Knopf I leaped with joy. Clutching the shabby typescript, I dashed for New York and Elinor, made a determined assault upon the Knopf office and finally saw Mrs. Knopf herself. I assured her that it was a magnificent book and that she would do well to publish it. She said she would read it and I returned to Ninth Street in a daze of happiness. We had a party that evening and Elinor somehow made everyone realize that I had a first book coming out, that it was a perfectly grand novel and that I had done it and made arrangements for its publication entirely without her aid, all by myself (with a helping hand from Mr. Mencken).

97

There were a frightening few days when I was not sure if the story would be taken, but a telegram came finally accepting it. I could not walk without dancing.

Elinor intended to write the novel about witches. She had thought of this idea for some time and had read a great deal on the subject which was not so very different from her studies for Casanova, or the Chevalier de Seingalt, who is de Langeist in *The Venetian Glass Nephew* but has a great deal of Cagliostro about him, somehow. These eighteenth-century descriptions of necromancy, demonology and witchcraft led her interest to the seventeenth-century pursuit of witches in England, the Basque provinces and New England, especially New England.

One of Elinor's ancestresses, a four-times-great-grandmother, was Mary Este, that unfortunate young woman of Salem who appears through all accounts in historical society papers like the *Topsfield Chronicles* to have been a most unusually noble young woman. The unfortunate Mrs. Este had a husband, several young children and led a blameless and busy life. But a neighbor's hysterical and epileptic daughter, ten years of age, said she had bewitched her, and as the cattle of other neighbors became ailing just then, Mary was tried and hanged on this evidence as a witch in Salem, leaving behind her a letter to her judges which is a short masterpiece of tempered calm entreaty. She begs the judges to investigate more fully the next time they choose a victim, for, although she knows their sincerity, she knows also her own innocence, and so fears that they may again be misled. Elinor knew this

98

document well, because we are all proud of our ancestress, although I have sometimes wished she could have been less saintly and a trifle more devilishly disposed in accordance with the rumor of her times.

Elinor's interest was there all along, and as her reading about the Massachusetts witch hysteria grew, she often spoke of the projected novel. In her poems she shows her passion for the New England scene, the cold granite of the characters and landscapes, but I think she intended a "Prinkin' Leddie" touch also to come into this book, a Merry Mount feeling, if that is not too hackneyed a term to use. Her erudition about such things as diabolic possession and necromancy was great and her infinite hours of research work seemed a pleasure, never a bore. She particularly disliked sloppy work about details, and so soaked and impregnated with a period and a place would her mind become that she would be just as careful to describe a coin or a button or a new tulip correctly as she would to mention the right date for the fall of Warren Hastings.

By the time a work was well started it became effortless for her because she saw the surroundings of the people she was writing about as actual, not vaguely imagined.

We heard a lot about this New England book, and I think it is a real loss that she never wrote it. Miss Esther Forbes' charming *O Genteel Lady* appeared just then with its delightful heroine, a sort of Margaret Fulley but with the looks and fascination that Margaret lacked, a writer from the Boston of the 'fifties who wrote of witches and Salem with a half-

99

supernatural gift but destroyed all her stories in a sudden revulsion from them. Elinor never destroyed her novel, but she never wrote it. Both by inheritance and through her own personality I feel that she would have been peculiarly fitted to produce a great story on the subject. As a matter of fact, she seldom, if ever, had to destroy work. By the time she started in on the writing she had so perfected the form in her brain that it came straight out of her imagination onto the paper without corrections being needed. Of course, her people would sometimes take things into their own hands, as every novelist has discovered in their work, but essentially the story was written and polished in her head first.

The clairvoyant perfection which distance gives to a writer appears in her description of the English countryside near Basingstoke and the hamlet of Camphile Eden when Gerald descends there in the opening chapters of *Jennifer*. She was four thousand miles away in America, but in spirit she helped Mr. Poynyard to furnish its charms with gallons of green paint and a gross of brass door-knockers, thereby slipping from her actual surroundings to ones even better known and equally loved. She knew exactly how the village looked and its houses were as clear to her as if she had been staring at her favorite house advertisements in a cherished copy of English *Country Life*.

Later on in England she wrote of America with the same close feeling and a love amounting to passion for the absent thing—in this case the laurel- and azalea-covered hills of West Virginia and on across the whole continent to the Pacific coast. The farther away the terrain the better she wrote of it, with the thrill of escape, of taking a flying holiday to far scenes and pleasant places. Last winter I tried to convince a man who had repeatedly read *Orphan Angel* with a particular passion for the western part, that Elinor had never been in California. He wouldn't believe me. She must, he felt, have seen the coast and the mountains. I tried to explain that she could project herself any distance and write of the Sierras when confined by influenza to a room in London, but he was scarcely convinced. She saw so many places in her short life—Canada and Carcassone, Stuttgart and Rome, Somesville and Biarritz—but she never reached the promised land where she sent Shiloh. . . . "Doubtless there is a Place of Peace."

CHAPTER

❖ IO ❖

THERE had been a number of flatteringly good reviews for *Jennifer Lorn* in England, where an unknown book by a new American writer seldom attracts attention. Quite soon Elinor was in correspondence with various people in London, editors and writers who wanted to read more of her poetry and to meet her personally. *The Nephew* was a success, too, although English sales are not very large compared with American. There is, however, a *succès d'estime* over there which is as pleasing to a writer as it is rare. She wanted very much to go over and at last felt she could afford to do so, not giving up the New York flat, but taking a little time off in London, partly to work and partly to play. The change would be a great stimulant for her, before she returned for the winter.

So in the early summer of 1926 she started alone for England. There had been a party to see her off, but the boat she sailed on, the *Minnewaska,* was a very quiet one, and she loved this quietness, found it restful and soothing after New

York. She was so delighted with her little cabin that she wrote us in praise of its smallness and the compact practicality that made it as neat as a tea-basket. Her typewriter exactly fitted the top of the small table where she worked for long uninterrupted hours; the dressing table, the cupboard, the berth which was really a bed, delighted her; boats, she said, were much more luxurious than ten years ago. As a matter of fact, this was not particularly true, but she had come back to America in war time when all the better ships were being used for transport service, and the comfort of the *Minnie* was new to her. She was in a mood to be very much pleased with things. The accents of the stewards and stewardesses were delightful. She loved working until tea-time and then emerging. I heard later from an old gentleman on board, Sir Maurice Low, then correspondent for the London *Morning Post,* how gay she was at tea and dinner, how pleasant it was to walk around the deck with her. She was utterly delighted at the prospect of re-visiting England and thrilled when the ship approached Land's End.

It docked at Tilbury and she went to a small hotel *north* of Oxford Street, at which my twenty-three-year-old snobbism was shocked, a hotel unlicensed for liquors which had to be sent in, and this further crime made me even more disapproving. The hotel was very quiet with small inconvenient rooms, but Elinor did not seem to mind this in the slightest. It was run by kindly, well-bred people, it was inexpensive, and she was satisfied. Some visitor to New York had given her the address.

She was always rather ingenuous and trusting about addresses and would accept them gladly, even those of hatmakers and hairdressers, sacred beings whose addresses should be forever secrets to their discoverers. Having been swamped on a trip to Paris with many little bits of paper confided to me by friends, I had come to loathe addresses, and thought Elinor very unsophisticated to want them.

Early summer in London is delicious and unchanging. It is festive and inevitable, like cold salmon mayonnaise for lunch, or a tip from the waiter on the Derby. Nothing has changed and there is always that gay, slightly crazy, dressed-up feeling at going out to dinner and the theater with the sun still shining brightly on your evening frock and silver slippers. June in London is a mixture of garden party and unexpectedly successful fancy dress ball.

Elinor went out almost every evening and spent days doing things which were to her pure delight. She read as much as she liked without any other duty to stop her. She wrote poems when they came suddenly into her mind. She wrote on a novel when she felt like it, which was often, because, living alone with herself, she could actually begin to live with the people of her book for a part of her time without having this dream broken by Bill or me or a business engagement.

She made friends quickly with both Bloomsbury and Chelsea, and had sprees with wild or bright young Mayfair aesthetes who were in the twenties but not less companionable because of that. She made pilgrimages to see people who lived in suburbs, and she loved doing it, even long quite complicated trips by Underground and then bus and then taxi. They delighted her because this was London and she was going to see Mr. Machen, or Mr. Roger Ingpen, or some other person equally revered, and they would give her a wonderful tea with a long pleasant talk afterward.

Then she would come home through the late afternoon and take a bath in the bathroom down the hallway (the little hotel was all hallways and passages and steps), and go back to her room to put on a pale green metal tissue evening dress which had liquid gold lights in it, and, with fresh skin and eyes bright with enjoyment, greet one of the precious young men who had come to take her out. Or, if she were not en route to the theater with a young high-brow, there might be a party in Bloomsbury, a "lit'r'y" one like the parties she went to in New York, or rather, *not* like the Literary Parties in New York—that syllable and three thousand miles making a lot of difference.

At such parties she would anticipate a good deal of fun and get it, too, because some of these new acquaintances would regard her as an aborigine from a rude untutored country, who by some miracle wrote lovely verse and quite acceptable English prose about the eighteenth century. So clever of said aborigine, they seemed to think, because they were quite positive that this erudition had flowered on top of a beginning of "oh yeah," "says you," "Iz zat so?" and other bits of vernacular dear to the English heart as specimens of true Americana. In vain would Elinor explain gently that the English language was not unknown to her from her first

105

sentient moments, and that these terms, delightful perhaps, were new and comparatively rare. They would be politely skeptic, and Elinor, thinking this immensely funny, would be politely ribald.

She made friends she cared for deeply—Leonard and Virginia Woolf, who asked her to Dorchester, and the Powyses, who asked her to their cottage beside the sea in Dorset, and Edith Olivier, and several others. She liked to go to tea with Mrs. Belloc Lowndes who seemed a link with Elinor's last stay in England, when we had all read *The Chink in the Armour* with delighted horror and adored it all. She was sorry that she couldn't go to see Mr. Beerbohm on the Italian Riviera, for she had somewhat the same feeling about him. She thought the new people were splendid, but that some of the people she had known through their work in the past when she was quite young were now glad to meet her as the author of her work, was to her heart-warming, like the pilgrimages to the suburbs.

Elinor had an affinity with tea, the way a Persian kitten has with a saucer of cream. It went with her. She loved it fondly as a beverage, as a meal, as a social festivity. I don't mean that she did not like cocktails and wine or a whisky and soda; she did like them, but she needed China tea. It was part of her, as cigarettes are a necessity to me and many others. She drank it for breakfast, at tea-time, and finally she became really Anglo-maniac or rather tea-maniac and had it at ten-thirty in the evening. Champagne, Emily Clark says in *Innocence Abroad,* was ordered the night Elinor read aloud

106

UNDER THE CRAB-APPLE TREE

ELINOR AND HER BROTHER MORTON,
SOMESVILLE, MAINE, 1919

part of *Orphan Angel* to Emily in London; this was to do honor to Shelley, but Elinor secretly suspected Shelley would have preferred China tea.

She had collected a great many invitations for summer week-ends and house-parties. She had economized rather at the little hotel, and she felt entitled to blow herself to some new clothes and a trip to Paris. She was anxious to be under the winking pink arc lights again. Besides, my mother and I were in Paris with my brother Morton, and she wanted to see us.

Elinor had been to my tailor in London (I'm just as bad as others about giving addresses), and she arrived in Paris in a grey flannel suit with a plain dusty-pink silk blouse and a big rose-colored malmaison carnation in her buttonhole. As I went across the courtyard of the Continental to meet her in the blue dusk of early evening, I saw her looking around in her open-eyed short-sighted way, a little confused by a big light near her. I thought then how extraordinarily young she looked, slightly awkward even, like a very pretty girl who has just left school in chic new clothes, radiant at getting away but easily startled. She recognized me when I started running and came across to me, preoccupied as always with some extraordinary thing which had just happened, some slight little encounter which at the moment she could magnify into a whole *histoire.*

My mother and I had a table in the Colonnade. She ordered camomile which she remembered was *calmant pour les nerfs,* and a chicken galantine sandwich because she could remember how good they had been at this hotel in 1913. She had a headache from the journey, but ignored it. Did we know where to get clothes? Things had changed since she was last in Paris; she was not sure she could afford Premet, and Hallé was gone. Of course she had lots of addresses people had given her but perhaps Nancy . . . And of course Nancy, conceited Benjamin, knew much better places, and Mamma offered the wherewithal that Elinor might afford what she wanted. We sat until late looking out over the courtyard as the sky deepened, swapping stories and asking questions about her London experiences and my complicated loves, until it was time for her to go back to the very charming and correct little hotel on the Rue de ——, but I won't give the street; it is one of the few addresses which are worth keeping secret.

That first post-war visit to Paris of Elinor's shines out very clearly and glowingly to me. She naïvely missed having Horace, that super-Parisian American, to go with her to his favorite restaurants. At the same time she was firmly deciding that next year she would induce her well-loved William to come to Europe on his vacation, for it would be his first trip and she had much to show him. But there was a lot for us to do together, she and I. She came over every morning across the bridge to our rooms high up on the fourth floor overlooking the Tuileries. Though we plunged into an orgy of shopping, I see her best in the plain beautifully cut grey flannel (which I inherited that winter) and the rose or turquoise silk shirt—her young girl's face as ingenuous as Kath-

erine Mansfield's "Mouse." She was thirty-nine and she kept
on looking twenty-three.

Once she was delighted because two young English college
youths loping toward the Sorbonne had ogled her politely and
said, "She's English," audibly. The French were too civil or
too knowing.

It was exciting to unfurl a Sunday *Herald Tribune* in the
Ritz bar, early in the morning when it was still empty and
the potato chips undamaged, to find therein that *Roundabout*
was selling well and to rush home to the Continental, barge
in on my mother and Elinor and tell them this thrilling news.
Elinor taught me the delights of talking shop and was not
bored by my frenzies. We would go down to lunch in the
sunny dining-room where the food is the best in the world,
though not as publicized as in many restaurants, and Elinor,
temporarily deprived of the right sort of China tea, would
manage to blossom forth on the strength of two champagne
cocktails and a perfect lunch. I had had my hair cut for the
first time, very short and curly, and Elinor, who had had her
first bob in England in 1914, a Jeanne d'Arc cut, approved
mine now and made an engagement with my coiffeur.

We were deliciously preoccupied with things—nice, con-
crete, exquisitely pretty things which do not rend and bite you
like emotions or ideas, but are openly for adornment and the
augmenting of natural charms. Blue-green shagreen had only
recently arrived as a fashion. One day we went to Franckie's
and bought cigarette cases and lighters of that color, and
Elinor never thereafter abandoned it as her own for her per-

sonal possessions. She always kept on getting everything to match that turquoise blue-green, even her pencils for the rest of her life. I bought a present for myself from the anticipated royalties due to the heroine of my novel and asked Elinor's advice about my next book. She explained to me her requirements in the way of hand luggage for one very grand party, and we hurried off to a trunk shop where the high prices were justified and mitigated by the fact that our grandmother had dealt there. Unwillingly I gave the street number of the girl who made my hats, and Elinor came around that afternoon with Dorothy Parker and her small, rather sad little black Scottie, Daisy, who was offended by the hotel rules which obliged small dogs to wait outside with teasing page boys. All three of us went miles up the hill to order quite ordinarily pretty hats, which were made more thrilling by the difficulty in finding the atelier.

Elinor took my mother and me to lunch in the pretty little hotel and fed us on delicacies, including raspberries which are to me more than rubies or plovers' eggs. We met the smart soignée proprietress and her distinguished husband, who was in snowy linen and a high white chef's cap. (I think it was the year of Orpen's picture, or soon afterward.) He was magnificent. This hotel was an Empire doll's house which Elinor, with her fondness for the small and perfect, very much relished.

There was a little restaurant called Michel's, one of hundreds of such establishments, but popular with writers and painters, and there Elinor went for dinner very often, turning it into a "marvelous" place by her ability to make an idol of a pet preference. She felt sure it was unique. She sat until late outside a café just as we all often did, but for her the table on the *terrasse had* to be at the Deux Magots; we either didn't care or sat down at the Select as being the line of least resistance.

She very much enjoyed seeing Ford Madox Ford, whom she had known and liked in New York. They had written to each other and she had read his books ever since the pre-war days when his last name was Hueffer instead of Ford.

But you felt that she was on a visit to Paris, and not, like many Americans in the middle 'twenties, semi-permanent there. I spent an afternoon watching her order and try on several embroidered silk dresses, simple two-piece things in heavenly colors which were most outrageously dear. Each time she chose one it was, you could see, for some particular occasion or place that she visualized, some setting where it would harmonize and this setting was either in England or New York, never France or other more exotic places.

She had met again a school friend, and her English hus-band, and she praised this girl of whom she was genuinely fond, yet all the time I noticed Elinor edging nearer and nearer to a subject temporarily dearest to her heart, a family with which she was utterly entranced and infatuated. She was in love with each member of that family and adored talking about them, even in the face of my mocking ribald attitude which may have been jealousy.

111

"Oh, Elinor, you always think some people I never heard about before are the most wonderful creatures on earth," I protested.

Very likely they were, although I suppose their heavenliness came partly from the amber glow of the footlights she turned on to prove to my skeptic eyes their quality of heaven, and the rosy spot which gave them the most becoming tints thrown by her admiring and idealizing hand as chief electrician. Next to Shelley, this family became the object of her current worship, thereby slightly displacing Mr. Aldous Huxley who, after all, was just a writer; these angels did not even have to write to be Olympians.

They had once in the dark ages been in Washington when Elinor was a very young married woman, but I don't think she knew them then. Now, however, I heard so much about the father and mother, sister and brother and the mother's sisters and the house-on-the-river and their joys, interests and annoyances that I retaliated by making Elinor listen to a *very* complicated love affair of mine which was obviously drawing closer and closer to a sad finale. But she was a most sympathetic listener and did not laugh at me. I noticed that her frocks were chosen with an eye on the Thames background, at which I groaned at her for being soft and catering to the well-known English liking for quiet pretty clothes, not too obviously straight from Paris. (This liking for the pretty and the restrained the English women seem to discard once a year when they appear at Ascot in things which look like a cross between the dresses in a 1903 photograph album and a musical comedy bridesmaid's outfit. But usually the idea is "nothing conspicuous.")

However, Elinor's choices were really very attractive and her faint air of virginity went well with the new purchases. I was delighted to find the following month that she had secretly and surreptitiously "blued" about half of her remaining funds on two dresses and a wrap from Poiret, barbaric, metallic cuirass dresses and a wrap of deep vivid blue-green with a Kolinsky collar. They suited her madly and were twice as becoming as the embroidered "correct" garments, but these bright Poiret things were for two or three particular parties where she felt it was all right to be dressed up. She was as careful about when to put on her best clothes as she was to dress her heroine precisely as she meant to do. It was a visualization of a particular scene in both cases. I wish I could interpolate at this point a short sketch of Elinor's called "I Wish I'd Worn My Silver Dress!" It came out in *The New Yorker* and was re-published in their collected prose album of 1931, and it is very funny and typical of the author. No attempts of another can make fun of Elinor as well as she could of herself.

After a few weeks of Paris, Elinor returned to London with her loot and the doll trophies of several evenings at night clubs to decorate the tiny bedroom in the little hotel. The Poiret things would necessitate third-class railway fares on all her visits, but as everyone else did it, she didn't mind in the least and probably wouldn't have minded even if it had not been the custom. I think it was about this time she saw Frances Newman, but dates have a tricky fashion of running away from me when there is no accurate Elinor to shout at for them.

The next I heard she was dancing around Stonehenge or something, which quite embarrassed my stern sophistication when I heard of it in a somewhat garbled version. Later in London, taxed by me with this surely odd behavior, she gave several chortles and admitted it was partly true. We were having lunch together—I think at the Ivy—and there was a good deal to talk over between us. Elinor made pictures to me of her past weeks. She had been at Lady Grey's house in the country and it had been lovely. The very young and enthusiastic Stephen Tennant had persuaded his mother to invite her, and at first Elinor was scared and then ceased to be scared. Lady Grey was extremely nice to her and not frightening at all. The place was awfully pretty, the house divine, Lady Grey went around in a fascinating little electric motor chariot, just like an armchair on wheels, along country lanes at ten miles an hour. She did it because her heart was not strong, but Elinor could not help envying her, it was such a smooth gliding way of getting about. Alas, that motor chariots should be so expensive! (Here I giggled, thinking of Elinor statelily tooling down lower Fifth Avenue in one.) The children called their mother "the heap of roses" because she was so pretty. Elinor had been placed in a bedroom with faded flowered wallpaper in a daisy design, which had little

poems and things written on it by the children years ago
when they were home from school, and little pieces that visitors had added since. Mrs. Sacheverell Sitwell was Canadian
and lovely to look at. They had all gone to see Stephen's
cottage and have tea. And then one night they had all gone
to Salisbury Plain and hadn't exactly danced on Stonehenge
but more or less. It was spooky and shadowy and quite exciting.

I digested all this with great relish and interest, and then
talked about myself and whether or not to get married. Elinor said, "Oh, do," absent-mindedly, added, "But don't if you
don't want to," and tried to launch out on a long talk about
that nest of exquisite paragons on the Thames where she was
going the next day. With ill-concerned speed I regrasped the
conversation (for who wants to hear about the faultlessness
of strangers) and invited Elinor to dinner in Soho that night
with two English friends who were not, thank God, prospective fiancés of mine and were therefore all the more liked.
Elinor accepted but returned to tales about the Y——s. This
is one of the times when to call people the X——s or the
Y——s is at least fifty per cent. true. I shall always hope
to find someone sometime whose name will make it one hundred per cent. correct.

The reason I have used some names in their entirety and
skipped others is because I have tried to put in cold print only
the full names of those who either write or are connected with
writing, and therefore are probably inured to print and type
in any form.

115

We arranged to meet in time to dress for dinner, after chattering over coffee until we both were late. I think these conversations over that lunch table must have sounded a little like one Bennett sister talking to another, not Constance and Joan, but the characters of the peerless Miss Austen, Jane and Elizabeth, transposed to 1926.

Dinner was late and was a good deal of fun. Elinor had introduced me in New York to so many of her friends that it was pleasant to have her join my friends in London. We had a large round table in a frivolous restaurant, rather de luxe for Soho, and a very swell meal with unlimited champagne. Elinor and the older man, a very attractive aviator, unusually affable, made the more impressive appearance, but we two younger ones were extremely pleased with ourselves and hopeful that the other two would get a little bit tight. I remember seeing Arnold Bennett standing in the doorway posing as he ordered from an obsequious *maître d'hôtel*. We had seen so many newspaper pictures of him with dark hair that he was a little astonishing in the flesh. He was much taller, much fatter and more flamboyant than one had imagined. Above a large white evening tie his face shone rosy red, and above that was a high grey-white pompadour. He looked like a very amiable and valuable white cockatoo.

Elinor was going on to a dance at the house of a lion-hunting lady of title in Chelsea. Elinor herself looked a little like a handsome young lion with her thick tawny hair just washed and glowing with life, a mane which was most becoming. The younger of the escorts drove us to the garden

116

door at the corner of the King's Road, and she stopped to thank them for the dinner, to primp in a hand mirror and to ask us for reassurance on her sobriety of which she felt doubtful. But even if she were slightly tight as she feared, we hastened to assure her that she not only looked perfectly correct but as virtuous as Joan of Arc.

She waved to us from the garden path and disappeared inside, chill and unruffled, with only her blazing eyes and a pink spot glowing on each cheek to show for the dinner party.

That was a complicated evening for me, because I had to meet a future spouse at one o'clock when he left the newspaper office, and yet not arouse the suspicions of the super-suspicious aviator. However, I managed this swap-over of dates in the middle of the night, and returned to the hotel "with the milk." Elinor seemed glad to see me back when I woke her up, but mildly annoyed at what the night porter or the early rising manageress might think, although she herself was not cross and hoped I had enjoyed myself.

I departed for Bournemouth, where she promised to follow me in a week, bringing with her the galleys of *Orphan Angel.* She had wanted to call her red carpet for Shelley *Mortal Image,* but as Miss Cather was bringing out a book with the word "Mortal" in the title about the time Elinor was first discussing various ideas, Mrs. Knopf persuaded her to use *Orphan Angel* instead and keep *Mortal Image* for the English edition. Her publishers in England were now Heinemann's, although *Jennifer* had been brought out by Grant Richards in '24 in the original American sheets. I had heard

117

part of the new book read from the manuscript, notably the wedding scene in Kentucky, but I knew there was a great deal after this that I hadn't heard. She had poured out her immense veneration and love of Shelley into the book, combined with her passion for the period and the American continent at that time. This long and arduous labor of love could not have been written except with the enormous amount of knowledge which she had about her subject, as well as the imagination which lights the whole book. She had, I knew, made it as fantastic as possible in order to make it the more pleasing and amusing a tribute to her hero.

She told me that she was going to read proof while staying with us and promised there were Indians and excitements toward the end. Two or three of my favorites among the poems of *Nets to Catch the Wind* were about Indians. Elinor admired Indians in a slightly horror-struck way, since she remembered about the massacres with atavistic shivers.

It was the chapter about golden Anne and the Cheyennes she had adopted which Elinor read aloud to my mother and me one evening by the weak light of a small table lamp. The long strips of proof slithered from her lap and curled about her like snakes as she read, her voice slightly breathless, sometimes stuttering over a word, while in the person of Anne she laid tribute of white doeskin and white moccasins, of bright barbaric beads, of vivid adoration and a little gentlest teasing, of a great headdress of eagle's feathers, at Shelley's feet. And while she read you felt she loved him so much that she made him a present not only of an Indian suit for a little

118

boy, but of the American continent and its eagle for a great genius.

"People won't like it," she said to us. But she was mistaken.

Her ridiculous side galloped gaily forth next day when she was very late for lunch, so late that the dining-room was about to close. She dashed in, pale, preoccupied, her mouth pinched to the size of a threepenny bit, her eyes large and brooding. She asked us in tones of deep tragedy if there were any of the little lobsters left, the tiny Swanage lobsters she was so fond of, and if the best of the veal and ham pie had been consumed. Luckily there was a lobster left and plenty of pie, though not perhaps quite the best bits. But what, we queried, could have detained her fifty minutes past lunch time in a familiar and humdrum seaside town? Well, apparently the explanation was that some friend or companion of Mr. Shelley had snatched some relic, bit of bone or odd portion from his funeral pyre on the beach, and it was buried in the graveyard of St. Thingumy's church. So she had sat on a near-by grave and wept for an hour. This is very like the ending of the delicious "Life Story of Lydia Greensmith," and is quite true. . . . She relished the half-sized lobster none the less.

A train in southern England, except an express to London, never goes any place too directly or quickly. It takes its time and everyone's time and stops at strange little places where you change to a still slower one and so on until a taxi, a trap or your legs carry you to your destination. With the aid of

several maps, the hall-porter's advice and technical sugges-
tions from the aviator who was staying at the hotel, Elinor
started out to visit the Powyses on the Dorset downs next the
sea. Their cottage would probably have proved almost next
door if she could have taken a rowboat, but it was remote by
land. After several changes of train she found the cottage
was still three or four miles away, and I think the road to it
was rather informal. It had been a coastguard's cottage and,
once you got there, was very taking and lovable, thick,
white and sturdy. There were sunshine and cliffs and the
ocean bathing, and seagulls overhead and friends to talk to
quietly in the evening. She would slip a raincoat over her
nightgown to go out and look at the sea in the early morning.
The cottage was tiny and Elinor slept in a still smaller one
next to it. The young man who had lived there had recently
been drowned. Her hosts asked Elinor if she minded occupy-
ing his room or if she were afraid of ghosts. Her tender
poem, "The Coastguard's Cottage," is proof that she did not
mind the ghost, but minded very much the tragedy of the unknown youth.

Elinor liked to think about her ancestors coming from Somerset, for she had found a few sixteenth-century and early
seventeenth-century Hoyt graves in some villages on the bor-
ders of Dorset and Somerset. I thought this a little far-
fetched, but it did give her another reason for loving this part
of the world in addition to its having been immortalized by
Mr. Hardy and possessing many natural charms. When I
teasingly suggested to Elinor the following winter that the

name Hoyt was probably Dutch she was horrified and remained in tears until I confessed that I had invented this heretical blasphemy on purpose to be annoying and to stop any chats on genealogy.

After a visit near Dorchester she went back to London for her last precious weeks there, delighted at my mother's promise to give her the money for the rent of a little house the following summer. She was immediately occupied by her favorite pastime of reading the advertisements and scanning possible façades of bijou residences near the embankment in Chelsea.

I had a violent toothache and a wedding just then, and was married in St. George's, Hanover Square, on Elinor's birthday with Elinor present. We both had on beige spectator-sports clothes and felt very spectatorish, although my tooth ached so badly that I was not very bridal. Elinor went back to New York within a day or two and I settled in South Kensington with the toothache, the husband and a cat, and a slightly grim memory of the extra glass of champagne I had taken on the night we had dinner in Chelsea.

CHAPTER

◇ II ◇

"WHEN I was eleven we were no longer in that Victorian high-ceilinged house in Philadelphia, where 'The Skylark' first sang to me. It was September in Washington and the air was warm and sweet as if all the grapes and peaches of Maryland and Virginia had flavored it to my taste. I stood before the smallest bookcase in the library and from its shelves I drew Trelawny's 'Recollections.' The window was wide open; there was plenty of light and soft autumnal wind in the room. I did not move except to turn the pages. Even the black leather chair was too far away from the scene within the covers of the book. I stood quite still and turned the pages, and the curtains blew in at the window and a few golden leaves blew in between them."

Elinor wrote this in 1927. Thirty years had not blurred the mirror of her devotion. The passage of which this is an excerpt is a prose evocation of an emotion which seems to me not unlike "on first looking into Chapman's Homer." There was nothing silly about Elinor's life-long feeling for Shelley. If she was absurdly fond at times, she was deliberately so.

122

No one is foolish who tries steadfastly to follow out the principle of thinking of someone who is not dead to them. To think of one long dead as still alive, still beloved, assures immortality for the beloved spirit, partly by reason of its selflessness, for there is no hope of mortal gain in it. There is a high sanity almost religious about a passion which is not dependent on worldly events. With everything else in life more or less unsatisfactory, this feeling is at least inviolate. It hurts no one and often creates strong bonds of sympathy between several devotees of the same shrine. It opens a horizon to them which is never storm-wracked. They found deep friendships here on their common interest, and they seem not to mind being teased or twitted about their idol, in much the same way that a lover enjoys any excuse to bring in the name of the object of his dreams. It is easier to understand than spiritualism, and as a form of hero worship it seems to give the worshipers constant reassurance, as if their hero were indeed at hand, so well do they know the attitude and reactions he would have if he were with them. Amy Lowell loved Keats in that happy way. My sister had as much joy from the study of Shelley as she ever found in her life.

This, like all close relationships, had elements of humor in it, as if she liked to joke about her dearest feelings and be gay about Shelley's sometimes pedantic speeches which amused and warmed the cockles, as well as the secret places, of the heart. Her dedication to the long novel about Shiloh, who was Shelley, and his attendant clown, David Butternut, who nursed him for three thousand miles, is one of the nicest

123

double meanings I have ever known. The disguise of the chief character is openly thin; the chapter headings are all singing phrases from his poems. The dedication is as follows: "To Whom it may concern." I can imagine her as she thought of this, the half smile around her small, firmly closed mouth, the minute examination of her thumb-nail as if she might find a heavenly miniature painted on it, the sudden idea and the rush to write it down, the satisfaction at capturing another joke to amuse her protagonist and her readers!

She had spent a long time writing *Orphan Angel,* but she did her galleys in one night. The book was almost word-perfect in typescript. She was a recognized novelist as well as poet by this time, but she had never earned a great deal of money nor did she expect to. Circumstances, however, changed. *Orphan Angel* was taken by the Book-of-the-Month Club, and many thousand other copies were sold by the publisher. Elinor made about eight thousand dollars in one lump from this long, romantic, old-fashioned tale of adventure. She was deeply surprised and held her breath until she could really believe it to be true. There was the money in her bank account, and all over America in fifty thousand rooms the book was lying on the table under the reading lamp. This was achievement on a big scale.

It was grand to be back in the Ninth Street apartment with Bill and her friends after a long gay summer of holiday and work with lots to tell him and a feeling of well-being with which to start the winter. There were continual calls to the telephone and many invitations. She was chosen for the small

jury of selection by the Literary Guild which was beginning
to rival the Book-of-the-Month Club. She exulted in the
Poiret garments for the evening and spent many hours a day
in a wash silk dress with a handkerchief bound tightly around
her bright hair, answering letters which poured in from all
over the country. She was particularly proud of a fan who
was a convict in San Quentin. She never snubbed genuine
correspondents and never let the post accumulate until it went
unanswered. She promised to read many books and review a
few, until the place was soon piled with volumes sent to her
or brought home by Bill from his office. They read vora-
ciously and compared opinions.

I came back to America—to Washington—rather grouchy
at marriage and England. Elinor, although always sympathetic with me, was extremely cordial to my husband and took
him out to a couple of parties with Bill and herself. She seldom turned disagreeable to either member of a couple when
they were contemplating separation and divorce. She was
technically ranged with the one she knew better, but this did
not mean that she changed toward the other. She listened to
both and never asked them out together.

Soon I was single again in fact, though not yet legally, and
I resumed my visits to New York to see Elinor, but now was
released from the maidenly necessity of staying at the Junior
League. I stayed at the Brevoort which was just around the
corner from her apartment. When I got off a train, rather
travel-worn and grimy, and ran up the steps to Elinor's front
door I looked older than my sister, who would be leaning

over the stair railing waiting for me. I was haggard and
hollow-cheeked from nerves and losing four teeth, and I
talked in a husky whisky baritone which Bill assured me was
very taking and would set a new fashion and a record for
deep voices. This voice used to leave me after a few hours
with them when I had enjoyed myself and forgotten the
nerves.

Elinor had the fun of planning dozens of uses for her
money from the Book-of-the-Month. It reposed in the Guaranty Trust while she tried over various mouth-watering
schemes in her mind. This was a delightful change from
the days when she had worried ceaselessly about the mortgage, or the still more recent times when her earnings and
allowance went entirely to paying her half of their current
expenses. She could hardly decide what her first extravagance would be, although she wanted to get something fit-
ting as a memento of the book's success.

I was sitting in her back room late one cold wintry afternoon waiting with Bill for Elinor's return. It was getting
dark, and she was late. Finally she came in breathing hard
from excitement and the cold, and rushed up to Bill.

"I've got them!" she exulted. "I'll have them to show to
you tomorrow! They're mine!"

"They" were at first a mystery to me. Finally she explained. For years and years she had spent hours poring
over rare book items in catalogues, window-shopping for her
heart's desires. And now she had actually gone to a real sale
and bid in for two treasures which gave her more pleasure

than all the jewels of the Ind! She had purchased part of the original manuscript of *Prometheus Unbound* and a check from Shelley to Godwin, his disagreeable father-in-law. His own veritable handwriting was actually in her possession now. She had gladly parted with eighteen hundred dollars for these two scraps of precious paper and was starry-eyed with rapture. I essayed a feeble protest and joke and asked her, in the voice of a complete cretin, why she wanted to spend so much money, when the *Prometheus* was unbound and the check was canceled. But no jibes penetrated her armor of delight.

She showed us the little manuscripts, the following day, with tears in her eyes—handling them as if they were a saint's relics, which indeed was what she thought them.

I think she had more pleasure out of this extravagance than out of any other expenditure in her life. She did not live so very many years afterward, and I am glad she bought them on impulse since they were to her what a string of pearls or an airplane might be to some of us.

Soon after this we went out to a party in the big high-ceilinged studio of Philip Moeller who was another Shelley maniac, and Elinor drew Philip and Theresa Helburn into a corner to gloat with her over her treasures. There were a lot of people there I didn't know, people who impressed but intimidated me; so I sat down under a long refectory table in the dark shadows of a big sofa and waited for Elinor to finish. Scrabbling in my bag for a cigarette, I looked up and found by my side a very personable youth, much younger than any-

127

one else in the room, who was sitting there in the dark in a pose of conscious charm, looking at the passing ankles of the crowd with a superior air. We picked each other up. He turned out to be Dwight Taylor, a great pet of Elinor's whom I had heard about frequently. We sat under the table and sulked together. Dwight's attractive nose was out of joint since the arrival of the manuscripts, and he was sulking at Elinor's preoccupation with charms other than his own. He talked even more than I did, and for the most part about himself and the careers he might adopt, but was for some reason not particularly boring in this simple egotism. As I was equally self-centered we got along quite well by talking continuously about ourselves without listening much to the other's speech. Elinor and Madeleine Boyd and several other young-to-middle-aged ladies had made a pet of the personable boy and encouraged him by telling him that he looked exactly like David Copperfield, or pleased him still more by taking his tantrums seriously and scolding him. With nothing much to do except absorb our kind host's drinks, monologue about ourselves and comment from the security of the table on everybody else, we became friends. I arranged with him to do the jacket for my second novel, while he promised to take me up to Harlem at the very first opportunity as I had never seen it at all.

In order not to arouse the suspicions of his group of older lady friends whom he was most anxious to keep in with, we arranged that I should display a critical and carping attitude toward him and to everyone express the utmost scorn of his

CAPTAIN SOMES' COTTAGE, SOMESVILLE, JULY, 1919

LATE EVENING SUNLIGHT AFTER SUPPER

charms. I relished doing this a great deal, for Dwight seemed an annoyingly conceited youth when he wasn't there to disarm you, and by dint of deprecating him constantly, I grew in favor with Ernest Boyd, Bill and other gentlemen who were glad to have this whippersnapper devaluated to their wives.

When Elinor discovered that I was two-timing her by meeting Dwight on the side for various dancing dates, she did not seem peeved but thanked God that I was unlikely to faint on her best Dresden figurine, as to her fury his last dancing partner had done. She quite often valued fine porcelain above humanity. Dwight continued to sit at her feet and pour out the endless saga of his ambitions, but as she did not mind listening, everything was quite harmonious and I got a most attractive jacket design as well as a number of dances out of the three-cornered friendship.

It was always pleasantly small town, the life in the Ninth Street apartment. Even when you didn't know people, they became familiar from being discussed by several different friends. We compared notes about books and swapped impressions of their authors. We roasted the publishers, unless we were about to go to a new one or had been given a very good lunch by the old. It was somehow a pleasanter circle than one immersed in political interests, and if it was not particularly useful or interested in outside affairs, it was also not harmful to anyone and only casually, pleasantly malicious about one another.

Elinor thought me peculiar to read four or five newspapers

a day, but not being famous has given me unlimited time for this amusement which I still prefer to any other.

In January and February she wrote several essays for *Herald Tribune's Books*, edited by Irita Van Doren. She had not published a book of poems since *Black Armour* in 1923 but new ones were accumulating and by the following year she would have enough for another volume. She wrote "The Applewood Chair" for the *Woman's Home Companion* and was pleased with the illustrations and the type which that magazine had had designed for itself recently. *Harper's Bazar* bought "A Birthday Cake for Lionel," a story set between the mountains of Somes Sound, with Shelley as a worn and middle-aged aristocratic hermit who has undertaken to supervise the bringing up of two delicious young females. She liked this romantic interlude herself, picked Lionel as a name because she was fond of Lionel Johnson and chose Mount Desert as setting because no poet could resist the place. Heinemann were bringing out *Orphan Angel* under the title *Mortal Image*, with a jacket design that was most attractive.

As the spring approached Elinor did not feel very strong; headaches of terrific intensity shattered whole days, only wearing off toward night. Even following a regimen, a careful diet and lots of water, would not really lower that mounting blood pressure which had ceased to alarm her only because she had become used to its unbelievably high figure. It was often over two hundred. Elinor had suffered from these headaches for such years that she had almost come to accept them. As far back as 1914 she had been taken by Horace to consult Sir William Osler. Doctors had cautioned her against bromides, but those and China tea were the only things which brought relief. The most far-fetched remedies had been suggested, dating back to a medico in England who had sent two wriggling black leeches in a jar of water with instructions for use (they disappeared mysteriously—thrown away by an impatient hand). Elinor endured the headaches and even worked through them when she was able.

No matter how much one loves New York and is happy there in a busy life, the telephone, the letters to answer, the commissions for articles or an address in a hurry, the engagements for parties of a semi-professional nature, tell on one who has ever spent ten years of complete tranquillity out of the world. A busy and personally popular writer has as many dates as a debutante and at the same time must keep certain hours for work, which, whatever its joys and rewards, is certainly hard labor. With several engagements every day after four or five hours of concentrated work, the writer goes to bed and lies awake half the night planning the next work to be done; the brain is too busy to obey the body's summons to relax. Elinor was exceptionally happy but did look forward to late May when she would sail for Tilbury to take possession of the little house near the Chelsea Barracks.

I thought she seemed rather thin in April, 1927, but I had just pulled out of colds and gloom myself and with great resiliency bounded back to good health, ebullient spirits and curly hair.

131

I mix up dates sometimes but I think it was about this time that Bill discovered he could get away for a flying visit to Europe. Although we were in Europe a month ahead of her I didn't see much of them because she took him first to London. They saw a lot of people they knew there, since it was Bill's turn to be the visiting fireman. I heard he greatly preferred English breakfasts to French ones, except for the coffee, and in this I sympathized with him more than his wife who cared only for tea. When they reached Paris it was summer and they were out all the time, seeing Ford Madox Ford and many others, sitting outside the Deux Magots or dining with an uncle and aunt of Bill's who were permanent residents of Paris. Elinor, who was hoarding her money for some scheme, was not so extravagant about clothes this time. Bill was a little bit timid about speaking French and did not like to go around alone. His visit was lamentably short. After he left for America Elinor had Madeleine Boyd go back with her to London for a week's stay before Madeleine went home.

Elinor was alone in London by July. Although she had many friends they were scattering to country places, so that when she came down with a sharp attack of influenza in its most virulent form, there was no one to look out for her except her maid whom she had rented with the house. Elinor, luckily, was intensely fond of the English girl, and the maid took care of her with the greatest devotion during the illness.

Partly to lower the blood pressure and partly from carelessness she had eaten very little for too long. Influenza left her weak and shaky, unable to get out of bed for some time. Her friends, the matchless Y——s, still the objects of her warmest admiration, were very kind about visiting her but they lived out of town on the river. The circle of young highbrows were good to her and constant in their attentions, but several weeks of her precious holiday had gone in illness before she could resume the normal life in England which she so enjoyed.

CHAPTER

❖ 12 ❖

O N A very hot day in late July I came out of the dentist's office and looked around for a taxi. Big fat drops of rain were just beginning to wet the dusty pavements, and there was no cab in sight. I found one several blocks away and we started for Chelsea. The rain came in torrents, in sheets, in white, slanting zigzags of water which danced off the pavements. It was one of those very violent summer thunderstorms in London which have been known to topple a bus over and flood the subway stations. My cab was stopped for half an hour in an alley which ran water like a river. Finally I arrived at Elinor's doorstep after the downpour had abated to a sulky, steady rain.

Her agreeable English "general" (a maid who does all the work of a small place) had an umbrella for me on the doorstep, but even so I was drenched and bedraggled. Elinor, who had been looking out over the barracks from an upper window, was disappointed because I was so late, but she admitted that there was some excuse. I loved seeing the house, but we postponed an inspection until after tea, for she felt aggrieved at having waited half an hour for this delectable meal. We had it downstairs in a tiny front sitting-room. An enormous cat, rented with the house like the maid but equally happy in this adoption, played around and acted as foolishly as a very young kitten. When it performed antics between one's shoulders and lap, it seemed slightly silly. It must have weighed about fourteen pounds.

Like so many very small London houses the tiny rooms did not seem cramped. They are like doll's houses but perfect for their size. A small drawing-room and an even smaller dining-room on the ground floor with a kitchen back of it, a little parlor, a best bedroom and bath above, and two more bedrooms under the slanting tile roof completed the place. That huge cat could not have been swung in the largest of the rooms, but Elinor fitted into it beautifully. She even had a spare bed always ready for country mice on their visits to town. Her young friends rather liked sitting on the hearth rug in front of the fireplace. She knew a good many of them that year. The poor things had just been labeled Bright Young People by someone and they must have loathed the name which was applied indiscriminately to all kinds and a good many ages of young people. Aesthetes, hearties, actors, actresses, painters or athletes were all called by this tiresome term.

I sat around after tea and heard about the beautiful Rosamond Lehmann whose success in America made me very jealous, about a painter youth named Rex Whistler, and about

135

people who had names which seemed to me to have come out of books, Tanis and Clodagh and things like that, very exotic-sounding to the American ear. What was more interesting was to hear about New York from the letters Elinor received, and about the Paris Americans from the visit she had one evening from Eva Le Gallienne, who looked, Elinor said, like a very thin little kitten that summer. Miss Le Gallienne had been exhausted by a hard year in repertory and touring and had come to England to rest. It was the only time Elinor ever met her. She was very enthusiastic about Miss Le Gallienne after expecting to dislike her.

I heard some more about the family Y—— who lived on the river. I was able to agree with her on the charms of the river, at least, for I had just been on a visit and had gone out in an electric canoe, in the pale glowing evening, past the romantic ruined castle near the Y——s' house and along under the great dreaming trees farther up. Elinor and I both loved the Thames in actuality, in poetry and in *The Wind in the Willows*. The week after the tea together she wrote this letter:

"9, Cheltenham Terrace,
"August 6th, 1927.   S. W. 3.

"Darling Nancy,
    Please explain to Mama that this letter is to you because of the book." (She had just received one of the first copies of my second novel.) "I'll write her very soon. I have had the

136

'flu again quite terribly—really rather badly—with a rotten temperature every night for what seemed forever and I am still somewhat shaky.

"You have certainly turned the trick this time! The book is truly marvellous in my opinion. For the first time I am sorry that you are my sister that my praise might be more public. I hear from New York, however, that it has been splendidly received on all sides. Not from Bill, for he left there too soon but from other and impartial people. It deserves a great success and will have it, I'm sure, but far more than that, it is a marvellous piece of work for you to have done. It may be uneven, although *I* can't see it, but if it is, it is only because its high places are so high. Of course the 'Cruel Thames' part simply murders me!—but it is all good. Terence is adorable in spite of everything and Cintra a dear. I am sorry you didn't put a scrap of *me* somewhere in it, as there *was* a scrap of 'The Baroness' in Elaine but this is the only flaw I can pick.

"Bill sends you the enclosed. He is a bit annoying in this letter I send a bit of, isn't he?

"I have taken a tiny cottage at Burley from August 16th to September 13th when we sail straight into the equinoctial.

"I am here until the 16th, it's now pretty hot and I'll be glad to get away.

"Lots of love.

"Elinor."

This warm praise encouraged me enormously. I decided to "put a scrap" of Elinor into the next novel which I was trying to write. Luckily this very lightly sketched caricature pleased Elinor, and she laughed a lot at "Athene" when she read *Bright Intervals* in manuscript. . . . "Sweete Themmes, runne softly 'til I end my song." . . . Dear Thames was being deserted temporarily so that she could show Burley and her friends there to William.

She took the "general" from London to Burley and to the most microscopic cot imaginable; they lived very well there preparing for Mr. Benét's arrival, until which time they subsisted like a pair of field mice, chiefly on the kindly fruits of the earth. Elinor had almost given up eating meat when she lived alone, partly because of the high-blood-pressure diet. She relished a vegetable marrow with butter and pepper, waxy, boiled new potatoes and fresh green peas with a hint of mint, a dish of raspberries and cream, and a gin and tonic with very little gin in it. But as Bill was arriving at Southampton they gave orders at the butcher's, ordered in whisky from the Queen's Head and beer and ginger beer for shandygaff, large masculine cheeses and various virile touches.

Burley, as you know by now, is a very small scattered village in the heart of the New Forest. Four roads meet, and there is an inn, a village general shop with groceries, calico, bull's-eyes and mineral waters; a branch of a bank with premises nine by twelve, a watering trough, vast trees and a couple of driveways to little houses which, covered with roses and surrounded by canterbury bells, look decidedly like stage settings. There are also two lines of cottages, where Elinor had rented one, a brooklet in a ditch beside the road, a few ambu-

latory cows and a baker's cart which looks like a picture by
Beatrix Potter. It's not a metropolis like Cranford and luckily it is off the main char-à-banc routes, although the last time
I was there one bunch of bored and perspiring midlanders
were dismounting from their char-à-banc at the cross-road,
demanding aspirin and lemon squash and complaining at the
lack of amusements.

Bill was there two weeks. He met a great friend of Elinor's
from the days before the war and was introduced to Forest
ponies and clotted cream. Elinor slightly begrudged him
chops and whisky, but then she did this with me, too, always
throwing an anxious eye at the Plimsoll line of the bottle
after I had poured a drink.

Stephen Vincent Benét turned up for a very short visit—
just a couple of days. Rosemary was not with him. Elinor
sent my mother a snapshot of the tall Benét brothers in front
of the cottage, standing on either side of her. They look too
tall for the low doorway. Steve read aloud in the evenings
from the *John Brown's Body* galleys, not only to Bill and
Elinor but to this indigenous Burley woman friend who has
never forgotten that evening. Elinor was intensely interested
in the Civil War. Her "Miranda's Supper" was a Virginia
war story Horace had told her, about an estate at a landing
on the James River; he had often spoken about the place
which had a classic name, Roman, I think, and belonged to
one of his Virginia cousins. Steve had soaked in Civil War
history as a boy in an army post in Georgia and ever since.
Just before this visit to Burley he had spent a year on a Gug-

139

genheim fellowship, working hard on this immensely long poem. It has since that time outstripped in sales every other book of poetry in America, even Kipling's! The figures are something like one hundred and twenty thousand copies in six or seven years, an unheard of total for verse. I saw this in F. P. A.'s column this year and as I take that as a sort of Bible, it must be true.

Steve was always very pro-Confederate, which is a little surprising as he is the grandson of a northern general, but his boyhood years in the South may have influenced him. Because we thought the southern side got all the gravy and romantic trimmings, Elinor and I were always Yankee sympathizers—she, down to the Puritan marrow of her bones! But she did write a most entirely Virginian idyl in "Miranda's Supper"; and somehow in her four sonnets in sequence, "Wild Peaches," she makes me, at least, long for the Maryland scene, although it is the cool New England landscape she approves for herself.

My mother and I were leaving for America earlier that autumn than Elinor, but she was to sail for home soon after us. She came up to London at the beginning of September to see us off and to arrange to be in town for a few final weeks. Though there were friends in the country, there was in London the excitement of meeting other writers, of going to parties like George Doran's at the Savoy where the cream of the young writers appeared in their very best bibs and tuckers to adorn his festive and liberal dinners. Rebecca West was there. Not an intimate friend, yet she wrote after my sister's death perhaps the best of the articles about Elinor. Her vivid words painted a better picture than any other. Mr. Doran enjoyed giving Elinor dinner and listening to her sagas about her work. Elinor had not yet decided on the cottage to buy with her carefully hoarded Book-of-the-Month money from *Orphan Angel*. It was still in the bank in New York, while she turned over in her mind the respective merits of the New Forest, the counties bordering the Thames, and Salisbury Plain. This idea of settling in Wiltshire was comparatively recent, the result of knowing Miss Edith Olivier, author of *Dwarf's Blood*. They had met at Lady Grey's and afterward Elinor visited her. Miss Olivier shared her passion for Shelley; the friendship grew quickly, aided by this, which was always a passport to Elinor's heart. She decided to dedicate a book to Miss Olivier and to look for a little house in a village near her. But it was so pleasant to be able at last to pick and choose that she delayed making a final decision.

We had overnight, my mother and I, a small suite in the new Mayfair hotel, and Elinor, between engagements, came in to say good-by. There was a two-by-four entrance hall and a sitting-room, shaped like a piece of pie, that just held three people. It was decorated in cream-colored lacquer with jade silk curtains, Chinese-patterned lamp shades and small but squashy apricot easy chairs next to two windows that over-looked Lansdowne House garden. It did not seem quite real. There was no sound of traffic. Someone had sent a sheaf of malmaisons, spicy pinked flowers with pink and mulberry ruffles streaked with coral, like dolls' dance frocks.

141

Elinor stood in the doorway, looking tense. She pressed her small mouth to a button and her eyes dilated tragically.

"If only—if only I was at the age and stage for a honeymoon!" she said, almost sobbing. "This would be so perfect, this lovely miraculous tiny room!"

"There wouldn't be much room for the groom," I murmured; "he'd have to be rather small and very thin."

"But he needn't be around much," she said, sinking into a chair and admiring the cream wood paneling.

She had skipped tea and was delicately greedy. We had just finished cocktails, and her eyes filled with tears at the thought that she had missed them; so I stopped teasing and hastily rang for fresh supplies. There were soon champagne cocktails and very thin pallid little sandwiches, crustless and almost transparent, all of them made of either *foie-gras* or shavings of smoked salmon. As the sandwiches and drinks matched the luxurious little jewel box of a room Elinor felt quite happy and twice as hungry as if they had clashed with the décor. She gobbled up the trifles and explained that though the name "White Ladies" was attractive she did not care for cocktails made with gin and so would stick to a known drink. The White Ladies were very good in that hotel, and she rather regretted refusing them.

Now that she had made more money she was very generous and gave both friends and me coveted garments, new books and special surprises. I made a date with her for October in New York. I had a vague idea that I might be going to live there that winter and already I was fussing about possible rents, which in 1927 and '28 were unbelievably high. The Ninth Street apartment was, even unfurnished and on a long lease, very dear, but Bill and she shared the rent and certainly its big cool rooms were worth it. However, for a person not yet arrived who had to scurry around the Forties for work, it was too far downtown. I did think of that part of the world at first and when I got back spent several days at the Lafayette and the Brevoort looking for rooms, but it was hard to find a cheap place at all decently furnished. I used to come in very tired to her apartment and in return for listening to news from England she would harken to all my troubles and sympathize.

On my second visit she and Bill had unearthed a rumor which thrilled me with its possibilities. *The New Yorker* was to take on an ordinary weekly book-reviewer so that Mrs. Parker could concentrate on writing reviews of the books she really felt like doing. I rushed up to Forty-fifth Street and got admittance on the ground of being Elinor's sister and also because I had sold them one or two short pieces. After boasting about my capabilities I captured the job, starting at thirty-five dollars a week, which seemed munificent just for reading and writing about half a dozen new books a week. I'd have read as many as I could lay hands on anyway. The job raised me to the seventh heaven, restored my confidence and enabled me to break the news to Elinor that for the first time in several years, all of two, I was madly in love and this time with an American whom I intended to wed the moment I was free. He had no job and neither of us had any money, but we

143

had' already planned a march on New York. I had no furniture or household linen, so I planned to rent a completely equipped two-room flat. The prices asked for these were appalling. Elinor approved the looks of the fiancé. He was handsome, blond and cool-looking with a sharply cut profile to be proud of. Elinor said that after a long diet of intellectual features, he was a refreshing sight with his colorless grey-blue eyes, light hair, neat nose and collar ad jaw. Not that he was particularly unintelligent-looking, just calm and unresponsive. I thought this too marvelous and she found him an agreeable piece of furniture on Sunday evenings.

I had still to get married and settle into an apartment, and to prepare for this, I tackled the books. There were twenty or twenty-five a week, of which six must be mentioned and one or two really carefully reviewed. I told Elinor that I was rather terrified, never having reviewed before, but I hoped to bluff it through. She sometimes got advance books sent her even ahead of review copies and would tip me off to good ones. It seemed such a vast sum to be getting, particularly as the magazine promised a raise if the work were satisfactory, and Elinor showed me a shop on lower Fifth Avenue where the discards which would threaten to choke any small home could be sold for twenty-five cents on the dollar, a price which meant forty to sixty dollars a month extra.

We got married soon afterward. I sat upon my wedding night writing the next day's copy and dreaming of a nice apartment with every good quality and a rent that was reasonable. Strangely enough, I found one the next morning

144

from an advertisement in the *Times* and was living there within two days.

That winter I saw Elinor almost every day, and in between times we "visited" over the telephone, exchanging views on the price of spinach, the best color for silk stockings, the leading bootleg brand of Scotch and what husbands liked for breakfast. I thought New York was the most wonderful city on earth and possibly in heaven.

Coming away from *The New Yorker* office on Fridays with a pay check, I would cash it in the Guaranty, hurry into Schrafft's, order half a pound of hermits for my adored and elegant New England consort, brandy snaps and ginger snaps for Elinor, English muffins for both and guava jelly for myself. Nine blocks farther north I would pant upstairs and find Elinor waiting for me. We had tea at five-thirty even if this meant spoiling our appetites for dinner, and we kept it hot for my husband who got in at six. Tea seemed to go with the cold black crispy December nights; it hit the right spot when you had just come in from the streets where the snow crunched under the chains of the cars. My sitting-room was square, painted dusky-biscuit, with faded gay chintz and a good mantel and fireplace. The flat belonged to a darling Canadian girl off on tour in Australia. It was shabby and worn out in patches by her wire-haired terrier, it was infested with fat brown metropolitan mice, but it looked lovely at tea-time under the soft lamplight. I had the review books piled in heaps under the long windows, convenient for a reaching hand from the sofa under the reading lamp. Elinor would

145

finish tea, sit with me talking books until Ted came in, tease him mildly and go off to join Bill at some party. She would tell me not to be prejudiced against La Duncan's book as she had been, because it was *divine,* unclassifiable and utterly readable. I would groan that Dotty (Mrs. Parker) had picked *that* one, and Elinor would generously give me her copy.

It was fun giving dinner to Bill and Elinor after the many times I had eaten with them. I knew her favorites already and some of his, for he and I shared a liking for mundane things like steaks. Elinor would condescend to drink martinis of my making although she usually refused gin drinks— gin *was* pretty villainous in 1927—because mine were very cold and, although not awfully strong, were at least mixed fresh every round. I got an ice-cream freezer in the toy department of Stern's, and as I lived just around the corner from Hicks' on Fifth Avenue, Elinor and I bought a box of strawberries there at New Year's time and produced fresh strawberry ice-cream for four, or at least almost enough for four. Sometimes Bill was late. Once Waldo Pierce arrived with Elinor for dinner and annoyed both my long-nosed French cook and Elinor by nourishing his immense frame on an amount suitable for a butterfly. Vast adorable Waldo, the only person alive who could out-talk both Elinor and me, working together at the top of our voices!

When I got in jams, either grammatically (that it happens still is self-evident to the gentle reader) or over a matter of opinion because I did not entirely trust my own, I would telephone Elinor for reinforcements, and she would come up and listen to my weekly piece before it went in to the magazine. At Christmas we all had a lovely and economical time choosing presents from the elegant and varied assortments of books brought home by Mr. Benét and me from our respective offices which were in the same building. Every Sunday night my husband and I had supper with them, and sometimes if there was a visitor of unusually difficult temperament to entertain, we would be called in to lunch at the Brevoort and then spend afternoon and evening at Ninth Street, because Elinor was childishly partial and thought we would surely make a good impression. I was selling short stories very well that year and could afford taxis up and down between the two flats.

Between us we pretty well covered the town and could discuss, when we met, almost every person in literary or semi-artistic circles who was amusing. We shared a lot of friends and sometimes clothes until I started to have a baby, which fact I disclosed to Elinor long before admitting it to any other human soul. In fact I think she knew before I did myself or at least before I was fully aware of it. She was the greatest comfort in a way which surprised me. I was feeling soppy and sentimental and prone to go into ecstasies over impractical pink chiffon coaties or rosy pram pillows, and I could not believe that this was a normal symptom, since formerly I had been fairly hard-boiled and humorous. Elinor said at once, "Yes, yes, I know what you mean. You long for satin cushions and marabou for yourself and foamy christening robes of

147

lace and net for the impending child." Which was too true.
I had acquired a passion for "dainty" things both for myself
and the layette. I even thought an appliqué rabbit blanketing
too sweet. I managed to steer clear of Mr. Milne as I was a
fairly good book-reviewer but otherwise I let go, and Elinor
was the safety valve. I could gurgle to her and be comparatively human with others because of that.

Elinor had been suggested several times to *The New
Yorker* as the subject of one of their profiles. Finally they
decided to let her write her own, the only time this was ever
done, I think. She signed it with her initials, "E. W.," and
wrote it in a few minutes, or at any rate in an hour. "Portrait
in Black Paint with a Very Sparing Use of White-wash" appeared that winter. Its mocking gaiety was laid by readers
at the feet of several writers, notably the blameless Edmund
Wilson. The following week at New Haven an admiring
young Prof, who had read her work for years, protested
sharply to Elinor against the impudent fellow who had
penned the lines. Finally she gave in and admitted the
authorship.

I met Peter Arno one day crossing Forty-fifth Street and
asked him how he had done the amazing picture which ac-
companied the poem. I was a little in awe of Mr. Arno, but
I was very curious and had not yet asked Elinor about it. He
told me that he had felt rather frightened of the appointment
with my sister and had wondered just how to do her. She had
asked him to wait a moment while she fixed herself up, and
then she walked over to a mirror and started primping, rub-

bing a finger along her eyebrows and looking at her hair. In a few minutes, while she stood at the mirror, he did the sketch. It has been reproduced three times at least and it is a breath-taking likeness. It has her personality crystallized into a wash drawing. My mother and I think it more like her than any of her later photographs. Of course, it is exaggerated, but so was Elinor.

Her loyalty would make her take up the cudgels quite violently in my behalf even against a great friend. That winter in one of the great piles of books which I lugged home every week I espied a novel by one Thornton Wilder and rejoiced because I had liked *Cabala*. The book was to be published the following week and had a funny title, *The Bridge of San Luis Rey*. Perhaps I was in a bad temper, but it disappointed me because it was not more like its predecessor, and although I gave it most of my space I said that it was simple to be omniscient about the Peru of 1719 because no one else knew much about it. Mrs. Isabel Paterson—who has for Mr. Wilder what Mr. Alexander Woollcott had for Mrs. Fiske, an admiration which is pretty breathless—came out a few days later with a crack about an unseeing "reviewer who was no better than an illiterate peasant." Elinor exploded with fury at the attack on my erudition and taste. Although she and Isabel were very good friends, she was temporarily in a great rage. As Mrs. Paterson, just at that period, felt about Mr. Wilder's work much the way Elinor felt about Shelley's *Letters,* she could hardly be blamed for criticizing my lack of enthusiasm. I pointed this out, also that Mrs. Paterson hadn't

149

used my name although she *had* said "a reviewer on a weekly"; but this just added fuel to the flame, as I had hoped it would. Elinor was really quite angry. The funny thing was that Mrs. Paterson was right—I have no education.

Emily Clark had left Richmond and her *Reviewer* several years before for marriage and Philadelphia. She was now a widow with a nice big old-fashioned house there, and her own Virginian servants who are the best in the world. . . . Emily's food! . . . Her invitations were always accepted, and when she asked Elinor and Bill that winter for a week-end they gladly went off for it. Although Elinor was fifty per cent. Philadelphian by inheritance, the last time she had spent more than a day there had been for an Assembly twenty years before. She thought it very amusing to re-visit that incredibly well-preserved, utterly conventional city, which still keeps all the mid-nineteenth-century taboos, and yet be staying with a young woman who was not only an intimate with the same interests as herself, but who was only Philadelphian by marriage and therefore not steeped in that peculiar city self-sufficiency. Bill and Elinor had a grand time with Emily, and with various painters and writers who were super-Philadelphians but did not behave so; and on the last night, which was very snowy, they all went to a big supper party at the old family mansion of the Thingummys on Rittenhouse Square. Elinor enjoyed herself in her best silver dress and reported to us that Philadelphia party suppers were as marvelous as ever. She saw the host speaking to our family friend and lawyer. The host was saying:

150

"Tom, there are some rather funny artist fellows here from New York. Queer-looking chaps. I wonder who that odd-looking man with the beard can be? Some scientist or Red or painter, I suppose. I must find out."

The gentleman with the beard was a Mr. Biddle. True, he painted, but his fondness for painting had been known since he had gone to dancing school with cousins and children of the same old gentleman who feared his subversive features.

However, Elinor was not often away that winter. New York was very gay, and if it palled one could always go over to Hoboken where Chris Morley was planning his theater, or find, even nearer home, restaurants which were Russia or Turkey or Italy or Sweden. Elinor was a celebrity by now, although she did not seem so to Bill or the Steve Benéts or myself. She was finishing *Mr. Hodge and Mr. Hazard,* which is my own favorite of all her novels. It is a limpidly lovely, painfully burning book, entirely about England (and influenza and Shelley and her own 'flu-wracked self), but it was largely written during a crisp, cold autumn and early winter in Ninth Street. Letters were always flying back and forth between England and the apartment near Washington Square. She could evoke a hot June day at Marlow in an instant.

I remember once that winter a cable coming in from a young man of lather la-di-dah extravagant tendencies asking for author, chapter and verse for a certain quotation. Elinor cabled back the required information, without consulting Bartlett or an anthology. Her mind was a supple instrument to her touch, always ready to be unsheathed. It isn't impressive perhaps, but I couldn't remember things like that offhand.

She gave me the names and addresses of her two doctors, the general one and the gynecological specialist surgeon, and they always treated me with extra kindness, but I was so well that marketing for the flat, reviewing six out of twenty books a week, writing short stories and having a baby left me still feeling strong enough for a convivial evening. Elinor herself looked particularly well, not drawn by headaches or overwork. She was again writing poetry and had prepared *Trivial Breath* for summer publication, her first book of verse to be published since *Black Armour* in 1923, five long years. She loved talking to Edna Millay when that lovely creature paid one of her rare visits to town. She would show her the new poems or a Shelley manuscript and, in her own words, watch "the green eyes of a high lyrical poet fill with tears at the evocation of a spirit."

Writing poetry, which was to her the breath of life, had become almost a luxury now that she was so busy with prose. She could still find time to compose it in the tub or on one of her weekly expeditions to the hairdresser which an earthquake or any other act of God could not have persuaded her to forego. Why genius should be supposed to be untidy I don't know, since my most intimate acquaintance with it led me to find it fanatically fastidious. Elinor adored having her tawny thick hair washed and waved and brushed. She enjoyed dreaming away two hours at this grooming and adornment which took on the nature of a rite, and which we all

152

kidded her about. There was no way to make her break her hairdresser's appointment, but she would take you along and let you talk to her while the purification with suds went on, because she did not look like a wretched skinned cat during the process; she was one of those people who did not object to the pitiless exposure of the open circle at Antoine's in London. Apart from a tendency to match things up a little too exactly, she had very chic taste in modern clothes, but she looked prettiest in a silk wrapper with her newly washed hair in a cloud about her long white throat. She would let me stay in the cubicle throughout the shampoo process and display to every one later three or four white hairs as proof that she had no tinting or retouching done to this chestnut fleece.

153

CHAPTER

⋄ 13 ⋄

Yes, the winter and spring of '28 were gay, and most writers were comparatively prosperous, so well off that they could give parties or have parties given for them by publishers who were then grateful to their authors and sometimes satisfied with them.

Elinor, with a book of poetry and a novel finished, was free to go out a lot. There were tea times and hours after dinner at Blanche and Alfred Knopfs', listening to spirituals and piano music from a gleaming, smiling colored singer in a dinner jacket, the quieter, older Rosamund Johnson at the piano, lovely music filling the friendly room lined with the bright bindings of first editions, Van Vechten kind and witty as he leaned against the mantelpiece, and little Louis Golding explaining that his American stenog. *would* put "country gentry" when he meant her to put "county gentry." There were dinners with Julian Messner who let Elinor order just what she liked at the very grandest restaurant-speakeasy, and lunches with me at the literary publishing speakeasy

154

where we were sure to see Guy Holt or Elliot Holt, Lee Hartman, Horace Liveright or his minion, the exotic Maurice Hanline, who professed an undying passion for both Elinor and me. Or perhaps a few authors would get together in the same spot and give tongue to laments against the publishers sitting across the room. Bill or Helen Woodward or Ernest Boyd, again late with his piece, might come in.

Evenings Elinor saw other friends of hers and of Bill's, the Morleys, the Canbys, the Saxtons—the first two *Saturday Review* colleagues, the third, Harper's. And there was Dorothy Parker's group, Heywood Broun, Ruth Hale, Mr. Benchley, Mr. Woollcott, Alison Smith, George and Bee Kaufman, who were all brilliant. The Theatre Guild originators, Philip Moeller, Miss Helburn, Lawrence Langner, had literary as well as dramatic tastes. The Van Dorens were a whole family of friends; there was Joe Hergesheimer up from Chester, or Mr. Cabell from Richmond, or someone in from Chicago. . . . It was a busy life. There was the excitement of having *The Venetian Glass Nephew* made into an operetta. (It was not produced until after her death and ran only a matter of days.) There was the thrill of a letter from a Mexican movie idol who wrote from Darkest Hollywood to say he wanted to make a movie of the book—which would have meant a lot of money if it had ever come through.

My only experience of seeing Elinor at a large public tea took place that winter. It was a humdinger. The publishers and the Literary Guild decided to give a party for Trader Horn. Elinor was asked to play hostess to Carl Van Doren's

155

host. The unfortunate old trader, looked upon as a semi-imaginary character, an aged Ulysses, had been dug out in the flesh from some London purlieu and dispatched via the *Minnetonka* to New York. He was sent over first-class, and I heard was returned in a fairly damaged condition. The poor aged one, who had already a taste for drink, was sent back very much the worse for wear in a haze of strong prohibition alcohol. In fact his drinking was started on the boat before arrival, and reached a crescendo at Quarantine where reporters, movie men, publicity agents and ship-news photographers were let loose on the dazed old creature at the same time that many half-gallons were broached. For six days he was carted around New York to sight-seeing points and parties. Rumor had it that he never got around to changing his clothes during this time; perhaps he had forgotten his luggage. The excuse was that he had to be displayed to convince his readers that he existed. He looked like a Salvation Army Santa Claus the afternoon of the tea-cocktail party which was to climax his appearance. He had a large dirty Stetson hat, which he never took off, bewildered innocent blue eyes blurred with alcohol, a long white beard which became quite wild and tangled, and a rather dingy suiting. "Everyone" was at the party. They flocked around the Trader encouraging him to dance, to display scars made by enraged elephants, and to talk. Plied by a peculiarly strong punch he willingly complied with all requests. He was less scared of Elinor and Carl than of others and insisted on their sustaining him through a movie scene. He persuaded Elinor to cut a mon-

156

strous birthday cake for him. I must say he seemed to enjoy the party, although I felt Father Christmas needed to be bathed and brushed and returned gently to a quiet pub parlor corner near the fire. Elinor looked lovely in silver and was extremely kind to the old boy, but it was a trying afternoon. She finally took refuge with pretty Peggy Leech who appeared calm and cool in a corner protected by bookshelves. The heat from the radiators was stifling, and we all melted. I thought Trader Horn might explode at any moment. Elinor and I left while the party was still going full tilt, and went to our separate homes in the chill evening, slightly embittered against publicity methods. I got a taxi ride up to the Park, and Elinor and Bill had Ninth Street to take refuge in.

I suppose that all this going out was bad for the blood pressure, but it was hard to refuse invitations. She liked best going to dinner at Mario's with Bill and perhaps a couple of others, but this wasn't always possible. She liked thinking about the type and format of her books. She wrote often to Mr. Elmer Adler of the Pynson Printers about the making of *Trivial Breath*. She delighted in the really lovely jacket design for *Mr. Hodge and Mr. Hazard,* a stag with a lion clawing its shoulder. She planned another visit to England for the summer and made up her mind to come to a decision on the cottage she was to buy with her carefully saved money.

Trivial Breath was a collection of poems written over a period of four years or more, but Elinor was planning to devote the summer of 1928 to verse which was welling up in

157

her as it had three times before: when she was a girl in
1903-04; in 1910-12; then from 1918 until 1924. Now again
a spring of music asked to be released.

But she must always be planning a new novel as well,
although she knew the toil of novels and how hard it was to
wrest time from the prose for the poetry she longed to write.
She had an idea for a new book and played with it to herself
and to me. I spent many afternoons in her back room. I
would watch her work for a while, and then we would refresh ourselves with tea and Digestive Biscuits, which are so
much more toothsome than their name suggests. I was a little
frightened of a forthcoming trip to France where the baby
would be born, and was reassured by Elinor and by listening
to her talk to an Englishwoman who was sailing for England
even nearer than I was to the expected date of her baby.
Elinor was kind and comforting to talk to. With myself
slowed up and ponderous, I liked to listen to her rapid speech
and quick descriptions. She said the new novel was to be
more or less in modern times, the end of the nineteenth
century. It would be partly about the Main Line outside
Philadelphia. Elinor, with her amazing memory, could recon-
struct every detail of Rosemont in the '90's. I cannot remember all she told me, but I do remember that the heroine was
one of two girls belonging to the Moon family, "who were, of
course, first cousins of the Starrs," and that she was to be
named Ann and her sister Cynthia. Elinor had once as a child
met a young lady called Ann Moon and never forgotten the
name. Of course, everyone knew that Starr was a well-known

Philadelphian surname. The period was about forty years ago, when Bar Harbor was very smart and young ladies wore little flat sailor hats and skirts with twenty-inch waists to climb mountains for a sunset view.

I thought for a moment that this story was mentioned by Mr. Benét in his introduction to Elinor's short pieces of miscellaneous prose at the end of her posthumous collected prose. But the story he speaks of is about the Angells and the Damons and not my Starr-related Moons at all. Ann the heroine was fair, but not so pretty as her sister, and she was thought slightly alarming by dashing young gentlemen because she had attended Bryn Mawr for a year and professed to understand and even enjoy the romances of Mr. Henry James, including *Roderick Hudson*. I wish I knew more about this delicious story that I might give it here, but, alas, my memory holds only the flavor, the essential perfume, of the tale and none of the plot.

I sailed for France in late April with the promise of letters from Elinor in England and possibly of a visit from her about the time the baby arrived.

She arrived in England in mid-May and wrote my mother a letter about her trip from Southampton to London which is intensely lyric and pastoral. It was one of those fine sunny summers which England protests as droughts. The blossoming hawthorne lay white as a fairy snowfall over the May trees around every field. Great patches of gorse poured bright gold over the commons, the lilac bushes sent waves of perfume in through the open windows of the train, larks

159

throbbed ecstatically overhead in the pale blue English sky, and Elinor wrote nearly as ecstatically as a lark. Even London seemed flowery; she had window boxes on the façade of the little Chelsea house and her much-loved Edith, the English maid, was waiting in the doorway.

Next she wrote of buying summer dresses, shady hats and even a sunshade for some river visits, to the adored Formosa, and to another house near Henley. Marlow, Bray, Maidenhead, Virginia Water—she praised each reach, the dark smooth water, the great quiet leafy trees in new green shading the grass, and lifting up her heart with their dignified antiquity, their assurance of long life. She was almost as much on the river as in London. Although she meant to settle on a cottage in Wiltshire not very far from Salisbury, it was pleasant to think about one next the river. She found she could later on rent a tiny cottage in Henley, but now Maidenhead seemed the most attractive place. It was near the Y——s', and near a new object of admiration. Elinor's illumined gaze as always shed its own light on the admired ones until they seemed to her to glow with more than human radiance.

Her first letters were *joyous*—there is no other word for such rosy, jocund raptures over the country and her friends, old and new. They were so crammed with delight in life and the world she lived in that my mother wrote to ask her to be photographed at a favorite photographer's on New Bond Street. She replied from the country that she would the next time she went up to town to get her hair washed and have a look at the letters awaiting her in Chelsea. She was busy writing poetry, of which a perfect torrent was flowing, and she enclosed a poem in manuscript which was very lovely. Then my mother dispatched her from Paris the news of my little girl's arrival on a hot evening after a long burning summer day, and we waited to hear her congratulations, waited for some days. I was feeling weak and impatient in a Paris suburban clinic, and my mother was ill in the city.

Finally, when the baby was about ten days old, a note reached me from Elinor which was full of affection, but so short that I was amazed. The handwriting was nearly illegible. She finished with a line saying she was in such pain that she could hardly hold the pen, and that I'd understand from her letter to Mamma. This letter I saw the next day. Although the full import and seriousness of her accident had not yet occurred even to Elinor, and much less to others, she described what had happened as nearly as she could. She wrote, in an agony which had been lasting for several days, that she had felt faint at the head of a flight of nine polished parquet steps and had fallen, hurting her back. She was in too much pain to describe exactly what had happened and had to close because the doctor was coming. I don't think Elinor realized that her fall was connected in any way with high blood pressure and incipient Bright's disease.

Soon after this disturbing news came a letter from Mrs. Knopf, one of the few friends who went to Elinor in London as soon as they heard, in which she reproached my mother for her absence at this time. As a matter of fact, I was not recovering any too well from the confinement and as my husband

and my brother had both skipped home to America, the baby and I would have been entirely alone if she had left. Elinor understood this better than Blanche Knopf, who was so distressed to see her friend in anguish that she could not help feeling indignant with others.

Elinor herself next month told me what happened. She had been staying in a country house near Henley with a married couple she had recently met. Coming down the stairs at three in the afternoon to join them in the garden, she felt suddenly dizzy and hardly able to continue. At the head of the last flight on a polished wood turn of the stairs she tried to dispel the dizzy feeling, went suddenly faint and fell unconscious. She came back to consciousness only after several minutes to find herself in the hallway at the foot of the stairs, very badly bruised, twisted and hardly able to rise. No one was around. She could hear voices in the garden; apparently no one knew that a mishap had befallen her. Because she had an idea, possibly absurd, that her hostess thought her spoiled and even cowardly, Elinor got up, walked out and joined the garden group without at first even mentioning her fall. But the pain at her back and on her spine below the waist grew momentarily more excruciating. Someone noticed that she had gone as white as paper, as if the light in her were snuffed out, and that she looked as though she might faint. She spoke of the fall, understating how bad it had been; but she knew that she would have to get to a refuge soon because of the ever-growing pains. No doubt the host and hostess were not cruel but only rather dense; and if they failed to realize the extent of her hurt it was partly because she did not want to admit how badly she had been injured.

If the host had known he would surely have motored her up to London. Instead he put her in a carriage on a slow train for London without a corridor. Elinor, alone, hung onto an upholstered strap and wept. She was too weak to stand and could not lean back or sit except sideways. Every jolt pierced her. Finally, only half conscious, she reached home and the maid sent for a doctor. He found at once that she had dislocated and injured a vertebra half-way down the spine, and that there was also a fracture at the end.

She could not eat or sleep. A really bad heat wave, the worst in thirty years, was engulfing Europe just then and sent the temperature in London up to 96. The nights were hot, and noisy with the buses of King's Road thundering near by, and the smells of the open stalls along the King's Road were wafted in disagreeable waves all day long. Another doctor came in on a consultation and ordered an X-ray. The damage had been done, and nothing but rest could help her. She lay in bed in her little room composing sonnets. They make a part of the sequence in *Angels and Earthly Creatures,* which is among the half-dozen best sonnet sequences in English. Another, braver commentator has said they are better than any others except the incomparable Shakespearean sonnets. I could almost agree. At any rate they are good.

She was some weeks in bed, tormented by pain, twisted by sympathetic rheumatic and lumbar twinges, lonely and discouraged, feeling as if her beautiful summer were slipping

163

away from her while she lay looking at the ceiling, unable to see the river or the meadows where she had hoped to wander all day long.

As I have said, it was several days before she had the strength to write us about the accident and it was several weeks before I dared take the new-born baby across the Channel. As soon as we could we went to England, to the seaside, where Elinor was to join us for convalescence just as soon as she could travel. In the meantime the sensational yellower papers in America played one of their usual pretty gambits and shoved in a wild story about Elinor falling down the well of some stairs and breaking her neck, and another about her falling out a window and breaking her spine. My brother saw these rumors of her death and cabled frantically. I would think it an idiosyncrasy of American papers to distort stories so, but last week one of the most circulated English sheets gave front page and headlines to the story of my brother's death-bed, and when I 'phoned half-an-hour later he answered me—"Well and in the best of spirits."

Elinor arrived at Bournemouth looking pale but pretty, with quite a bundle of new poetry to show us. She seemed to recover pretty well although she still suffered more than she cared to admit. She had taken to smoking occasionally, since the fall, and somehow it did not seem to go with her.

My baby was, to be truthful, really rather remarkably pretty although very bald, and Elinor spent hours telling it so, which even at six weeks it seemed to understand. She would put

Edwina on the bed and poke her gently with a finger, cooing, "Pretty baby, oh, very pretty baby!" until the minute infant beamed all over. I have never seen Elinor take such a sudden liking to anything; she made more fuss about Edwina than I did myself. She liked to have her dressed up in her very best clothes, and as the baby was born in Paris these were rather exceptionally fine. I don't know how much Elinor usually cared for brand-new infants, although I do know she liked small children. She gave me news of several contemporaries of Edwina expected just after I left New York. One was George Doran's grandson, a most bonny young gentleman who was also Mary Roberts Rinehart's grandchild and the son of Elinor's friends and mine, Mary and Stanley.

Her feeling for Edwina seemed very personal, perhaps because she had given me much encouragement all winter and spring and felt she'd had a hand in the whole thing. We bought the most preposterous bonnet and coat for the baby at Steinmann's on Piccadilly as a present from Elinor. They were most outrageously expensive. The cap, a tiny Jacobean bonnet of point lace like the ones Van Dyke painted on Henrietta Maria's children, was too grand to wear; but the coat, as long as a christening robe and as expensive, made of snow white camel's-hair with a China silk lining, was worn and worn. It was washable and I have seen it draped or floating like a banner on most of the docks and railway stations between Paris and New York. Elinor pulled out several white fish-foody paper notes to pay for these tributes so that Edwina would look in early youth at least like a princess. As a matter of record she has turned out to look somewhat like Elinor.

When she came to Bournemouth, we heard many of Elinor's new poems, the finest she had yet written. And I in turn, reminded by Elinor of my promise to put her in a book, read as far as I'd gone in *Bright Intervals*. The title came from hearing the B. B. C. announcer mincingly pronounce the weather report over the radio: "Weathar will be raineh, with some bright intervals." "Athene" was a caricature and supposed to be funny, which luckily Elinor found her, but I was charged with seeing that when the character recited her favorite John Donne I should change it to something less hackneyed than "Go and catch a falling star," and this I forgot entirely to do.

Elinor got an advance copy of a novel written by an acquaintance in which the chief character—an abominably fake sort of prig—was physically at least sketched from Elinor. She was amused more than annoyed although naturally she could not continue to waste much affection on the author of this rather offensive story. But sometimes she loved being identified with a character if it were in a story by someone she cared for, such as *Tin Wedding,* by Margaret Leech, which has a poetess in it I thought not unlike a mixture of Elinor and Edna. Since she liked both the book and its attractive author, Elinor hoped my idea was true and felt flattered and amused.

After we got the ceremonial baby clothes and before Elinor returned to Henley, she sandwiched in another visit to Burley which is particularly lovely in early September. The common is covered with heather, the bees are busy making strong dark amber heather-honey, blackberry fool is served for luncheon every day in orchid and heliotrope whirls of cream which look exotic, and the cottage gardens are full of neatly frilled pink dahlias. She stayed with Mrs. D—— and her daughter who had named her first little girl after Elinor. Feeling temporarily somewhat stronger she persuaded them to motor over to Chilmark with her to see the cottage. Not that it would be possible to convert Hampshirites to Wiltshire as a preferable spot but just to share the pleasure of her own place.

Because she had been ill for just the weeks she had been wanting to go to house parties, she enjoyed now going to the London branch of Poiret's and ordering several very splendid dresses. There was one particularly lovely (I am afraid she never wore it), heavy ivory moiré, perfectly plain except for some gold and silver thread embroidery, stiff and archaic like a church vestment or a medieval cope, with a long scarf of vivid rose red. Just having the dresses hanging in her cupboard cheered her, and besides, she meant to dazzle us with them later in New York. They were of beautiful materials and she felt as if they were coats of mail, armor against the world when she would put them on.

She had half finished the short novel about Miss Moon and was going to read it to Miss Olivier and to me when she next saw us. It was gay and ornately perfect, a prose version of *vers de société* which was openly meant for diversion. The writing of this book had been sandwiched in between her po-

167

ems, affording a relief which suited her better than idleness. She was in too much pain to enjoy a holiday given to reading and lazing without work, and the novel afforded her some distraction. It was rather necessary and certainly desirable to get serial rights for it because there was the Chilmark house to be furnished—and how she would love that job!—and steamship fares soon eat up royalties. She thought perhaps Charlie Towne of *Harper's Bazar* would want it when it was finished. She had not yet realized that to complete her book of poetry she would need several more months of solitude. But she knew in her own heart that *Angels and Earthly Creatures* was much her finest poetry, so that she felt an unusual eagerness to see it in print.

CHAPTER

⋄ 14 ⋄

ELINOR left Bournemouth to visit Edith Olivier at Daye House, Salisbury. There she was sure of a warm welcome from her charming and vivid friend who had many of the same interests as Elinor and a very indulgent attitude toward her. Miss Olivier knew Wiltshire well, for she had been born in an enchanting Georgian rectory at Wilton and had lived in other places there, including the delicious village of Teffont, before she settled at Daye House. Elinor drove about with her and also explored on her own for miles around. Her hostess lived inside the great wall of Wilton Park in a small grey cottage that I should call Strawberry Hill Gothic which had once been the dairy of Wilton House. This gay little house was peaceful and quiet, hidden by the wall and enormous trees but it was only a moment or two from a busy highroad and very near to Salisbury as well as to the precise charms of the town of Wilton.

But Elinor fell in love with the reserved and subtle, even shuttered beauty of Chilmark village which is really at the

169

back of beyond. It is about nine miles from Salisbury and is off the main road, reached by lanes frequented by slow contemplative cows, half hidden by hedges and clumps of trees in a hollow of the Wiltshire downs. Perhaps she was first attracted to that part of the world because William Beckford had lived near there in the eighteenth century—the man who built the various Follies and wrote *Vathek*. Elinor liked eccentrics. Or perhaps it was the row of cottages in an unbroken line but with thatched roofs of different heights that was the magnet.

There was a miniature "grand" house, no bigger than a bandbox but quite manorial, at Chilmark cross-roads where two lanes met but that one was too expensive for her. Finally she decided on a grim and rather fascinating Elizabethan cottage at the side of a byroad—one of Chilmark's side streets, so to speak—a cottage built of that prevailing slate-grey Wiltshire stone in the sixteenth century.

Chilmark is built on the vast quarries of the Romans, and there still are quarries in use near it. Hers was a long grey cottage with a thatch almost the same color and a secretive garden wall of the same stone, much too high to look over, but as the house is built on a little rise a person standing at the top of the garden could look down and over the wall. Across the road was a gardener's cottage, also thatched, and surely that was the smallest house in the world! It had a front door and windows in both stories, mullioned windows at that, but Elinor would have had to employ a dwarf to take care of that part of her domain and only very dwarfish children could have stood upright on the second floor. The cottages needed a good deal of renovation, and this she planned to have started so that the place would be ready for occupancy by the spring of 1929. Then she wanted a Baby Austin so that she would not be entirely cut off from humanity. It was a great joy planning this life, down to details.

Teffont, with its houses all along one side across a brook, appeals to me more than Chilmark. But in the latter one has a sense of being curled up in the very heart of England, part of its kernel, very far from the madding crowd. Chilmark is reputed to have a population of three hundred persons, but to the casual eye it looks as if thirty at most lived there. Teffont, no bigger and quite near on the map, seems, because it is on a main road and has a very lively little brook down the middle, infinitely more in the world. The water in this brook, Miss Olivier told me, is reputed the finest in Wiltshire. She had it so from a very old receipt for a lotion given her when she lived there.

The contrast of this part of the world with the almost urban amenities of the river bank was profound. But it was Elinor's final choice of a home, made after viewing and pondering all sorts of possibilities all over the southern part of England. In the meantime, while the house was not yet ready to be occupied she would go back to her little place in Henley where Bill was coming for his holiday.

Poetry was pouring out of her this summer in spite of the continual pain of her back. At Daye House her room in the trees, with the round open window called the porthole, look-

171

ing straight into green leaves, and the two arched windows
with sliding shades from the dairy days, rested her eyes in
beauty, and she wrote a great deal. Two unpublished poems
written for Miss Olivier and printed here for the first time
are included by the courtesy of their owner who showed me
the originals in Elinor's hand, rather blind and scribbly from
her constant suffering but quite clear. I felt such a start of
delight at this totally unexpected pleasure that I knew other
readers of her poetry would want to see them. These two
songs were written at a time between working on the sonnets
of her sequence in *Angels and Earthly Creatures.* They are:

BIRD SONG
I.
Little Clock

Half-past-four and the first bird waking,
    Falling on my heart like a thin green leaf.
If you are alive, your heart is breaking,
    If you are dead, you are done with grief.

Half-past-five and the birds singing sweetly,
    World washed silver with the rain and the wind.
If you are a saint, you have lived discreetly,
    If you are a sinner, you have surely sinned.

Half-past-seven and the birds singing madly;
    Sun flames up in the sky like a lark,
If there are things to remember sadly,
    Wait and remember them after dark.

and "Little Prayer" which she first titled "Holiday" and then
scratched through the word.

> My best content were death:
>   Yet let me have
> A lightly taken breath
>   Above my grave.
>
> Content I cannot win
>   Save by that sleep,
> Yet count it folly and sin
>   Living, to weep.
>
> Permit me, while I live
>   Still to be gay,
> Till Thou consent to give
>   True holiday.

So, after a very happy time with Edith Olivier, seeing, too,
near-by friends like Stephen Tennant and Rex Whistler and
Cecil Beaton, who also was planning to settle in Wiltshire,
she went back to Henley, and the last chapters of her short
life began to hurry her toward her end.

William was due very soon from New York, and Elinor
and her fond Edith prepared for him, rather, one judges from
her letters, like two herbiferous animals expecting one of the
larger carnivora. Probably they did no more than tell the
butcher to send a sirloin and a leg of lamb every week as well

as the usual four chops and small roasting fowl, but to hear Elinor describe her preparations always made me think of a picture in the hall at home called "Ye coming of age in the olden Tyme." I visualized roast oxen, tuns of beer, barbecues and massive kegs of whisky. It is true Bill had a normal appetite and could hardly be expected to live on buttered vegetable marrow with a dusting of pepper as Elinor could and did, but the exaggeration was due simply to the excitement of providing for a masculine hunger in a purely feminine home.

One of the greatest pleasures Elinor and Bill shared was reading to each other in the evenings, and now for the first time in years she had a whole sheaf of poems to read him. This thrilled her because, though of course she knew they were good, poems are like hot sealing wax in that they really do seem to need the impress of a good listener and critic to set them properly. It was with a good deal of palpitation that she read them to him and noted how genuinely he was startled by their astonishing perfection. She had lived poetry for weeks at a time; now they all were shown to him, the harvest of months. It was Bill, I think, who first heard her plan and helped her plan, to have the Sonnets printed at a town printing shop in Henley, for their own delectation. He knew that she felt she had more to write of this particularly fruitful vintage and so did not press her to hurry back to America as he would ordinarily have done. She could not just yet interrupt the music which she heard.

He was friendly with her new paragon, Mr. X——, who

was the host of the house where she had fallen so disastrously, and liked his wife well enough, although I imagine he was able to restrain his enthusiasm for any of Elinor's shining lights. For they were usually just quite ordinary everyday people on whom the beam of her wild unbounded admiration would fall, lighting up to radiance their quite unexceptional features for a little while until it flickered and turned elsewhere. Perhaps she remained most constant in her fondness for the Y——s but in the autumn of 1928 Mr. X—— nearly displaced them. Elinor had no illusions about the mental attainments of her pets; it was that they were different from other mortals, of finer clay, even when they were a little bit stupid. They trod the boards of her imagination bathed by becoming footlights, and were not obliged to do much thinking. On the other hand, we, her family and her friends of the literary world, were all required to keep up to an impossibly high standard of wit or be scolded as witless.

Elinor rather hated to see Bill leave. She could not leave with him and perhaps jar to a stop the whole delicate mechanism of her work, but she would miss him dreadfully. I also was going home with my baby and my mother, and I wanted her to come back to New York again so that we could have another winter of close companionship. But she would stay on, although it was getting cold and damp with river mists and very lonely now that the gaiety of summer crowds had all left the river. She came up to say good-by to us and we sat in the Mayfair drinking side-cars, surrounded by huge plush dogs which were a generous but ill-advised tribute to

175

my three-months-old baby from Rosa Lewis. A young man who liked me and admired Elinor's work (he was too fastidious to read my books) came into the bar to say good-by and to meet Elinor. She felt a little bit bereft, having us sail away while she stayed on and worked, and decided to drop in to see Rosa whom she had never met, because Rosa would remind her of wild Americans and their wild ways and she was getting somewhat homesick. Mrs. Lewis at this moment swam into sight with a chiffon scarf and two white Scotties trailing her, masses of flowers in one arm and a champagne glass in the other hand, with which she punctuated her remarks, all criticisms of the 'otel and the 'otel management. Elinor did go and have lunch with her twice and was, on that very short acquaintance, the only woman that the redoubtable Rosa ever mentioned as a mixture of angel and Joan of Arc.

After we had sailed, she went sadly back to Henley, to work as hard as she would have worked at the MacDowell Colony. She found difficulty in sleeping and would walk seven and eight miles in the open air to tire herself so that she would get a few hours' rest. Later she gave me two little tweed skirts, short and flaring, that she slipped on with a jumper for these walks. They are beech color, brown as autumn bracken, and look just like her.

One morning in October, very cold and damp, she woke up with a start. For a few minutes she could hardly breathe, she was so frightened. One side of her face seemed entirely paralyzed, and although the area diminished when she felt it, there were several inches on her cheek and near her mouth which had acquired a sudden terrifying rigidity and insensibility. In the mirror the spot did not appear very conspicuous or ugly. It had a slightly ironed-out, smoothed look. On the other side of her face, still normal, there was a slight grimace, a wrinkling of the facial muscles to balance those smooth few inches, which gave her a faint involuntary smile, ironic and a little superior. She was naturally brave, and so she did not at first make a great deal of fuss. Trembling slightly, she called her maid who sent for the local doctor. Ill-advisedly or not, he told her it was facial neuralgia, a bad case of facial neuralgia, and this Elinor used to repeat as if reassuring herself, although I don't think she believed it for a moment. She knew, I think, that it was a stroke, although she never did realize that it was a second stroke following the first one which had resulted in her fall.

She went to London and the doctor there could give her no hope of the partial paralysis passing off quickly, but neither he nor the local doctor nor Elinor herself expected any sudden fatality. She felt she must put up with the inconvenience and even the anguish of this little quirk in her cheek, this unwanted grimace, for many years. She wrote to us understating things as much as possible, but cried that her vanity, her precious vanity, was irretrievably wounded. I would not call her exactly vain ever; she was too extravagant and possibly eccentric a person to be commonly vain. But something was deeply wounded in her; she felt helpless in front of the unexpected attack, like a child a little bit frightened of the dark. She was not frightened of death; it seemed to her noble and of a

177

great peace not to be found elsewhere; but she was frightened by new traps and snares as yet undiscovered, placed by Life.

Suddenly feeling alone in Henley in spite of the Y——s and the X——s she went to Miss Olivier and found that the deep beauty of the Cathedral and Close, the shadows on the downs and the kind voice of a real friend helped her to bear this new alarming trouble.

The relentlessness of fixed holidays occurred to her when she realized that she had promised to be in New York to spend Christmas with Bill, and then see the rest of us as well. She felt bound to come over although what she longed most to do was to hide in these rolling uplands in her own little grey cottage, lying like a smooth mouse against the hills around Chilmark; to recuperate the spirit in silence; to read and work a little bit, alone except for the friends near by.

Again and again we have said, her family and friends, that it was better to have her snuffed out suddenly than to live on partly invalid. But I think this is a way of whistling in the dark to keep up our courage, for Elinor loved best of all to work and her finest work was often done when she was ill, in Boston in Peter Brigham Hospital, in New York, in London and in Henley.

Now that I have seen Chilmark I feel that there was something prescient in this choice for a refuge of a little easily wielded house, old as the trees and stones. Her bright spirit must have loved the sleety grey of the stone, the slippery shining mouse-colored thatch, all in the black pearl mono-

THE LITTLE COTTAGE AT BURLEY HAMPSHIRE, ENGLAND, 1927

STEVE BENÉT AND ELINOR   BILL BENÉT AND ELINOR

THE BARN GARAGE

tone, the water grey of the New England which she has sung in verse and praised in her prose works and her letters. Chilmark—the name itself is cool and sharply chiseled like the stone from its quarries—was the matrix from which the spirit in her forebears had gone out and wrestled with our own country. It was not a soft easy place, lush and facile to farm and colonize, but bleak and enduring. The house she chose and the walls of its gardens have not broken or crumbled in four hundred years. When it was being built out of the very ribs of England, her ancestors were leaving to build the ribs of America on the New England rocks. She could have lived there with integrity and joy.

She did not seem sick with life, only transiently unhappy, but one felt her unhappiness would pass like the shadow of a cloud over the wheat, like the wind over the grasses, and leave again a happy landscape.

From the small but ever constantly reiterated point of view of the looking-glass the ironic smile, fixed as on a statue, would not have seemed disfiguring to the observer in the glass had not the observer been herself. She felt a real terror at facing New York, thinking of it as New York and not as the home of genuine and really affectionate friends. Had she thought of meeting on her return individuals and not a great frightening body, she could not have minded; for indeed she was scarcely aged or altered to the intimate eye, and to enemies she had only to exaggerate slightly the smile to a sneer as if to say, "Aha, it's not half so bad as you hoped it was, and aren't you sold!"

179

The area affected was just about where one would put rouge; it felt, she said, rather as if she had put on a large and stiffish beauty-patch or made a small criss-cross of sticky plaster.

Taking all her courage in her hands, but leaving behind her in England her maid, most of her manuscripts and almost all of her books and dresses, she booked her passage on the *Aquitania*, sailing on the first of December, and at the same time promised herself to be back by the middle of January to superintend the changes in the interior of her cottage. Miss Olivier arranged to meet her at Southampton when the *Aquitania* should bring her again to England.

Elinor first went back to the Old Cottage, Henley, to collect a few clothes and the completed manuscript of *Angels and Earthly Creatures,* which was to be delivered to Knopf in New York, and to give Edith directions about her imminent return and the subsequent removal to Wiltshire.

CHAPTER

◦ 15 ◦

Some time in early November when I was settling myself, husband, baby and maid into one three-roomed flat I had heard from Elinor, in a very toned-down letter, of her facial paralysis. This news, even couched in her understating words, was a great shock to me. She was such an immaculate, clearly outlined person as well as so exceptionally pretty, she was so soignée by nature, such a burnished person, that a flaw seemed incredible.

I had two more letters from her, one from Wiltshire and one from Henley, both so full of the strain and pain co-existent with leaving England that I felt tempted to write, "For God's sake, darling, don't come back if you feel that way about it! Don't come until you want to." But the sense of duty, always exaggerated in one when resistance is low, seemed to force her to come, although she faced the project with real anguish and kept cutting down the time in America to less and less. It seemed to be partly that she dreaded New York and the demands on her, the social demands and those connected with her work, which would surely engulf her, and partly that she hated leaving just when she wanted to plan the arrangement of the new domicile. If it had been the country she was facing and no strangers, just perhaps Edna and her husband, or Somesville where the snow hid the town safely in winter ermine, she would not have minded so much. But she flinched from busy Christmas and New Year's weeks and the parties.

I heard from my mother and Bill when her boat would dock. I got my husband to bring me a pass and was on the dock on a bright, bitterly cold December morning when the *Aquitania* came in. It was always a bit of a job getting away from my apartment early, what with a baby of a few months and a talkative French cook, but I made it in time. Elinor was one of the last persons off the boat, but from the vantage point near the gangplank where I stood shivering I could see her talking to two of the junior officers and looking extremely well. When she reached me she had tears in her eyes and her eyebrows were quirked with the effort of trying to laugh instead of cry. The paralyzed cheek looked and felt perfectly cool and smooth when we kissed, but the other side of her face was drawn and a little dragged at the corner of the mouth with fatigue. Her steward had been particularly kind to her during this rough winter passage and now he soon had her small pile of luggage together, piled up waiting for an inspector whom I fetched from the desk. Elinor promised to be back in one of his cabins on a return trip in three weeks' time, and the man ran off and left us alone.

182

She was very brave and gay and I was completely flabbergasted by her face, because it was so much less disfigured than I had expected and dreaded. Although her natural stiffness and expression of primness were now set into a slightly more rigid mask, her face was still remarkably pretty. The torture was that she was always conscious of the muscles.

"It's like a thumping big shot of novocain and a bad mauling at the dentist's, only it doesn't wear off," she said.

"But it hardly shows at all!" I exclaimed.

Elinor shrugged and smiled. "But think, darling, how you fuss if there's even a tiny spot or scratch, and this never stops."

By tacit consent we referred to the paralysis as facial neuralgia. She sat on her calf-skin hat-box cracking jokes with me, talking in that eager rush of hers and full of a lively interest. I groaned with fury because she had been prevailed upon to bring over a pair of pseudo-oriental bedroom slippers to post to Mrs. X——'s mother in Cleveland. They were awful-looking pink things with pom-poms which, although dutiable so that we had to unwrap and show them to the inspector, were so shoddy that he waved them away with a scornful smile. Elinor was always doing preposterous errands like that for people. She had brought with her only hand luggage for the few weeks' stay, and we were soon finished with the customs. Bill arrived breathless just as we were leaving. I had already given news of him, of my baby, my mother, my elegant husband and of Marjorie, Elinor's handsome and lovable colored maid who was eagerly awaiting her. Marjorie,

183

I knew, would baby her and keep her from missing England too much. Elinor had been up since dawn and although we arranged to meet that evening, she went to bed instead and I promised to come down the next morning.

As a matter of fact in that small flat busy with the baby, the marketing and a good many articles and short stories, it was terribly hard for me to get away at all early, but I managed to be down at Ninth Street by noon the next day. We had so much to talk over. Marjorie fixed coffee for me and tea for Elinor, purring at having her again in the sunny back room. The poems, many in manuscript, some in typescript, and various notes to the publisher and printers, lay over the wide deal work-table. She read me several poems and promised to show me all of them at the end of the week when she had them in order, ready to deliver. She was, she said, curiously exhausted and had felt quite worn out the night before, but this I put down partly to the tiring ordeal of landing and the docks. We were very happy to be together again and went uptown to lunch in my favorite literary-speakeasy which knew how to make shads have roe and asparagus have stalks entirely out of season. It seemed in the dark room lit with pink-shaded lamps as if we were two years back and I was up on a spree from Washington. Elinor explained that if she kept on feeling so tired she would not go out at night much but would get Marjorie to stay later and fix dinner for Bill and herself. There was lots to read to him and tell him about.

We were quite frivolous at lunch and had cocktails and liqueurs and passed literary back-chat with the tables in other cubby holes. We swapped details of contemporary grand passions, mine being still an infatuation for the neat-featured husband, but I had achieved being friends again with the young publisher of several years ago, which amused Elinor. She told me about her waning admiration for a gentleman in England and talked lots about Chilmark, how I would love it, how the baby and I could squeeze in with her, or perhaps she would arrange the miniature gardener's cottage for guests and I could have that. "But it wouldn't be grand enough for Ted—besides he couldn't stand up in it." We planned the parties we would have with beloved Miss Olivier whose books I would like, and with Stephen and Rex and other Wiltshire worthies. We sat late over our coffee, and then I had to go back to the apartment to be sure the baby hadn't tumbled out of her crib.

Edwina, who usually screamed at visitors, again beamed and gurgled at Elinor. And Elinor was surprisingly fatuous about her in return, as if there had never been such a young female before. But Elinor had a thundering headache which had been creeping up on her all day. I can remember fetching a box of aspirins which the baby grabbed and strewed all over the floor. Elinor went quite white and fey with pain. I made her take a taxi home instead of a bus. After she got back she rang up and we chatted over the telephone companionably for some minutes as the headache was finally receding.

Next day I managed to get away and join her from two till four, while she went to the hairdresser's, and that night she

185

felt strong enough to dine at Mario's near her apartment with
Bill and Ted and me. She wanted to talk over the new half-
finished novel for the *Bazar* with me, because I knew Mr.
Towne perhaps a little better than she did.

She saw Mrs. Knopf but not many others that week. I was
a little bit insistent on taxicabs because she sometimes went
wan and worn-out. Doctor Connie Guion, her physician for
several years and a good friend, too, dropped in to see her
about the headaches, and Elinor went uptown to pay her a
visit at her office. Elinor was working in the evenings on a
final arrangement of the poems. Daytimes, when she was too
tired to come uptown, I was commanded to join her down at
Ninth Street. Several days passed while she fixed up the typescript of the new novel to show to Charles Towne. We rode
around town in a taxi toward the end of the week doing a
little Christmas shopping and talking about this book which
lay in her lap, a neat pile of typewritten pages. She promised
to let me have it very soon, but she rather wanted to take it
to Atlantic City with her in two days when she went down to
see my mother and stay overnight with her. Elinor looked so
tired that I took her home to my place and fixed a drink while
she played with the baby. After the cocktails I went home
with her in a taxi, promising to keep our usual Sunday night
date which we four had observed faithfully all the preceding
winter.

Elinor called me at about half-past eleven on Sunday morning to say that the poems were all ready for the printers, and
that she had been writing letters all morning after finishing

186

the arrangement of the verse. She was a little bit exhausted but would telephone me that evening, and we might have a very late Sunday supper near by or bring it in to her flat. This was on the sixteenth of December, 1928.

I was reading when the telephone rang at about eight—or a few minutes later—that night. I heard my husband say, "Oh, no!" and knew something had happened. I took the receiver. Bill, weeping, told me that Elinor had asked him for a glass of water, and when he brought it to her she had said, "Is that all it is?" and had fainted. But she had not fainted. She had been sitting reading, and suddenly, like a light extinguished, her life had left her. Beside her was the orderly pile of poems bound with two elastic bands, ready for the printers on the morrow. "Doubtless there is a place of peace." I hope she has seen Shelley plain.

THE END

POEMS BY ELINOR WYLIE
FROM HER FIRST, PRIVATELY PRINTED,
BOOK, "INCIDENTAL NUMBERS"

TO PAOLO AND FRANCESCA IN PURGATORY

O fair pale shadows of a love long dead,
    I look into your eyes and see no tears;
Your brows are calm; your hearts that burned and bled
    Have learned still peace with the long opiate years.
Lethe's cold flow has quenched your souls' hot pain,
    And the great flaming glory of your love.
Only dim shapes and memories remain,
    Reflections of the bright fierce world above.
Through chill Eternity can ye quite forget
    That silent time upon the edge of night,
The hush of ecstasy when your warm lips met
    Your rebel spirits' rushing Heavenward flight?
Cannot the past your frozen breasts inspire
    To flashes of the old sad splendid fire?

Summer of 1902.

THE FAIRY

The folk of the valleys
   They are not my kin,
They walk in cool alleys
   Green gardens within,
Through closes of roses
   And orchards within.

Their feet are submitted
   To pathways secure,
My footsteps have flitted
   From lure to bright lure
Of rillsides' and hillsides'
   More perilous lure.

My sisters and brothers
   They dance on the height,
We hear one another's
   Wild songs through the night.
They hear me, and cheer me
   Through all the long night.

Upon the white heather,
   Beneath the white moon,
They dance all together
   Unto a sweet tune,
So airy, a fairy
   Alone hears the tune.

Some midnight when mortals
   Are sleeping I'll win
My way past the portals
   Of cloud to my kin,
And meet them, and greet them—
   My magical kin.

On the moon-whitened meadows,
   That look to the sky
Like silvery shadows,
   We'll dance, they and I,
With laughter, hereafter,
   Forever and aye.

Summer of 1909.

"INHERITORS OF THE RELENTLESS SWORD"

Inheritors of the relentless sword,
The bright, indomitable sword of mirth,
Dedicate from the instant of their birth
To struggle with the dark powers; they have warred
Against great odds, light heartedly, and poured
A radiance of laughter on the earth,
A flaming beacon amid bitter dearth
Their shield must burn—to loose the high-strung cord
Or sheath the blade were treason; they must leaven
The whole sad world; their courage may not cease;
They must give battle seventy times seven;
But at the last they shall have full release,
And Joy shall lean from out the Gates of Heaven
To crown their tired brows with leaves of Peace.

Spring of 1910.

FEAR

Some sentinel upon the farthest hill
May see their tattered banners through the haze,
Some sudden dawn may set their spears ablaze
Their rust-red swords may catch a glory still
From some great sanguine sunset; or they will
Steal on us some deep night through devious ways,
In darkness marshalling their dim arrays,
And, striking in the silence, strike to kill.
The fresh-hewn granite of our strong defence
Lifts our emblazoned pennons to the sky;
We know not where they hide their huddled tents,
In what grey fens and misty vales they lie,
We wait the hour they scale our battlements,
Their haggard eyes alight with Victory.

Summer of 1910.

EVE IN HEAVEN

Eve, the mother of us all,
  Walks in Heaven alone,
Jostled towards the outer wall,
  Shouldered from the Throne,
Souls remembering her fall
  Think upon their own.

Angels multitudinous
  Shun her steps, and so
Saints and martyrs scorn her thus,
  Praying as they go;
And, "The woman tempted us,"
  Cry the damned below.

From her side the seraphs start,
  Lest her touch defile;
Modestly she goes apart,
  Silent all the while.
What has she within her heart
  Telling her to smile?

Still she smiles, nor envies yet
  Crowns nor grace thereof
No—nor Saintly Mary set
  All the saints above,
Never shall her heart forget
  Eden and her love.

Sometimes even she will stare—
    While the pæans roll—
At the Virgin crowned and fair
    Whom the heavens extol,
Thinking, "She was never there—
    Ah—poor soul, poor soul!"

April, 1911.

THE KNIGHT FALLEN ON EVIL DAYS

God send the Devil is a gentleman,
  Else had I none amongst mine Enemies!
  O what uncouth and cruel times are these
In which the unlettered Boor and Artisan,
The snarling Priest and smirking Lawyer can
  Spit filthy enmity at whom they please—
  At one, returned from spilling overseas
The princely blood of foes Olympian.

Apothecaries curse me, who of late
  Was cursed by Kings for slaughtering French lords!
Friendless and loverless is my estate,
  Yet God be praised that Hell at least affords
An adversary worthy of my hate,
  With whom the Angels deigned to measure swords!

May, 1911.

198

YOUTH AND SORROW

A little while we saw her weep;
A little moment after
We watched her spirits lift and leap
Upon the wings of laughter.

Above the level of the crowds
She sees new footholds shining;
And, look—she dances in the clouds
Upon a silver lining!

August, 1911.

SEA-BLUE EYES

A QUATRAIN BY ELINOR WYLIE

SEA-BLUE EYES

I stare at you, Ianthe, since you ask,
  Because your eyes look, brimmed with fervid blue,
Like disks of crystal in a tinted mask
  Which the intense Ægean gazes through.

Somesville, Maine, Summer of 1919.